The Financial Times Guide to Technical Analysis

The Financial Times Guide to Technical Analysis

How to Trade Like a Professional

Jacinta Chan

 Pearson

Harlow, England • London • New York • Boston • San Francisco • Toronto • Sydney • Dubai • Singapore • Hong Kong
Tokyo • Seoul • Taipei • New Delhi • Cape Town • São Paulo • Mexico City • Madrid • Amsterdam • Munich • Paris • Milan

PEARSON EDUCATION LIMITED

Edinburgh Gate
Harlow CM20 2JE
Tel: +44 (0)1279 623623
Fax: +44 (0)1279 431059
Website: www.pearson.com/uk

First published in Great Britain in 2011

ISBN: 978-0-273-75133-5

British Library Cataloguing-in-Publication Data
A catalogue record for this book is available from the British Library

Library of Congress Cataloging-in-Publication Data
Chan, Jacinta.
  The Financial times guide to technical analysis : how to trade like a
professional / Jacinta Chan.
      p. cm.
  Includes bibliographical references and index.
  ISBN 978-0-273-75133-5 (pbk.)
  1. Technical analysis (Investment analysis) 2. Investment analysis.
I. Financial times (London, England) II. Title. III. Title: Guide to
technical analysis.
  HG4529.C446 2011
  332.63'2042--dc23
                                2011024731

10 9 8 7 6 5 4 3 2 1
15 14 13 12 11

Typeset in 9pt Stone Serif by 30
Printed by Ashford Colour Press Ltd., Gosport

Contents

Acknowledgements / vii
Publisher's acknowledgements / ix
Preface: what makes an exceptional trader / xi
Some traders' terms / xvii

PART 1 WHAT DO TRADERS KNOW? / 1

Introduction: the market technicians / 3

1 Know the market: how to read and construct charts / 9

2 History has a habit of repeating itself / 30

3 Spot the bubbles and win / 44

4 Follow the winners: trading with the trend / 51

5 The tools that professionals use / 64

6 Leading technical indicators in the market / 72

7 The profit opportunities / 85

8 Wave after wave / 95

9 Booms and busts: risks and returns / 100

10 The secret / 106

Conclusion: leave the random walkers busy with their arguments – the market technicians are busy making money / 112

PART 2 TRADING WITH PROFESSIONAL TECHNICAL SYSTEMS / 117

Introduction: the trading game plan / 119

11 Technical indicators to use / 125

12 Principles of a technical algorithm trading system / 132

13 Understanding market characteristics and what to do / 139

14 Simple formulas to design your own trading models / 146

15 Programming trading rules into your system / 152

16 How to write a good trading plan / 157

17 Losing a little to gain your capital / 165

18 Practise stop loss / 169

19 Fine tuning the trading wheel / 173

20 The total trader – winning trading psychology / 178

Conclusion: the complete trading set-up kit / 183

Getting started / 188
Glossary / 193
Bibliography / 202
Index / 213

Acknowledgements

The body of technical analysis knowledge did not happen overnight. It is built up over a century by great traders and technicians who have put together their knowledge to form what we know today as technical analysis. Therefore, the first acknowledgement goes to the founder of technical analysis, Charles Dow, whose observations still hold true today and benefit many traders such as myself. There are many great contributors to technical analysis, too many to be mentioned individually here. However, there are some authors whose works must be mentioned: H.M. Gartley (1935) for *Profits in the Stock Markets*, Richard Arms Jr. (1999) for *Profits in Volume: Equivolume Chart* and Gerald Appel, the originator of Moving Average Convergence and Divergence (MACD). One of the greatest technical indicators contributor of all time is Welles Wilder, the author of *New Concepts in Technical Trading Systems* and originator of the Resistance Strength Index (RSI), Directional Movement Index (DMI) and Parabolic Stop-And-Reverse (Parabolic SAR). Other leading technical indicator contributors whose works are mentioned here are George Lane, the originator of Stochastics; Woods, Vignolia and Granville, the developers of On Balance Volume; and Ralph Elliott, the originator of Elliott Waves. Other great technical analysis teachers of all time whose work greatly influenced my thesis and work are John Bollinger (*Bollinger on Bollinger*), Larry Williams (*The Definitive Guide to Futures Market* (Volumes I and II)) and Perry Kaufman (*Trading Systems and Methods*).

Credit is to be given to Equis International whose Metastock software is very useful for profit analysis.

This book did not happen overnight either. It took the efforts of many individuals from different backgrounds and parts of the world whom I have come to know as friends over the years. I thank Dr. Noor Azlinna Azizan for going through this book. I thank Christopher Cudmore, my commissioning editor, for publishing this book and all the team at Pearson Education. I thank all my friends, my colleagues, clients and readers whose support make my books bestsellers. I thank all my family, especially my parents, Chan Kok Heong and Yap Chin Tuck for their love and support. Lastly and most importantly, I thank God for all these wonderful family, friends, colleagues, clients, editors and the great teachers of technical analysis who contribute to the success of this book.

Jacinta Chan

Publisher's acknowledgements

We are grateful to the following for permission to reproduce copyright material:

The Financial Times

Figure 1.0 from FTSE100, *http://markets.ft.com/markets/interactiveChart.asp;* Figure 1.1 from FTSE100, *http://markets.ft.com/markets/interactiveChart.asp;* Figure 1.3 from FTSE100, *http://markets.ft.com/markets/interactiveChart.asp;* Figure 1.5 from FTSE100, *http://markets.ft.com/markets/interactiveChart.asp;* Figure 1.10 from FTSE100, *http://markets.ft.com/markets/interactiveChart.asp;* Figure 2.1 from Nikkei 225 *http://markets.ft.com/markets/interactiveChart.asp;* Figure 2.2 from DJIA, *http://markets.ft.com/markets/interactiveChart.asp;* Figure 2.3 from SSE, *http://markets.ft.com/markets/interactiveChart.asp;* Figure 2.4 from ASX 200 *http://markets.ft.com/markets/interactiveChart.asp;* Figure 2.5 from ASX200, *http://markets.ft.com/markets/interactiveChart.asp;* Figure 2.6 from ASX, *http://markets.ft.com/markets/interactiveChart.asp;* Figure 2.7 from *http://markets.ft.com/markets/interactiveChart.asp;* Figure 2.8 from Hang Seng *http://markets.ft.com/markets/interactiveChart.asp;* Figure 2.9 from Nikkei 225, *http://markets.ft.com/markets/interactiveChart.asp;* Figure 2.10 from ASX200, *http://markets.ft.com/markets/interactiveChart.asp;* Figure 2.11 from *http://markets.ft.com/markets/interactiveChart.asp;* Figure 2.12 from DAX, *http://markets.ft.com/markets/interactiveChart.asp;* Figure 2.13 from CAC40, *http://markets.ft.com/markets/interactiveChart.asp;* Figure 2.14 from Nasdaq, *http://markets.ft.com/markets/interactiveChart.asp;* Figure 2.15 from Eurofirst300 *http://markets.ft.com/markets/interactiveChart.asp;* Figure 2.16 from Dax, *http://markets.ft.com/markets/interactiveChart.asp;* Figure 3.1 from Hang Seng, *http://markets.ft.com/markets/interactiveChart.asp;* Figure 3.2 from Hang Seng, *http://markets.ft.com/markets/interactiveChart.asp;* Figure 3.3 from Hang Seng, *http://markets.ft.com/markets/interactiveChart.asp;* Figure 3.4 from Hang Seng, *http://markets.ft.com/markets/interactiveChart.asp;* Figure 3.5 from Hang Seng, *http://markets.ft.com/markets/interactiveChart.asp;* Figure 4.1 from Nikkei 225, *http://markets.ft.com/markets/interactiveChart.asp;* Figure 4.2 from Nikkei

225, *http://markets.ft.com/markets/interactiveChart.asp;* Figure 4.3 from Nikkei 225, *http://markets.ft.com/markets/interactiveChart.asp;* Figure 4.4 from Nikkei 225 using Moving Aver, *http://markets.ft.com/markets/interactiveChart.asp;* Figure 4.5 from Nikkei 225, *http://markets.ft.com/markets/interactiveChart.asp;* Figure 4.6 from Nikkei 225, *http://markets.ft.com/markets/interactiveChart.asp;* Figure 4.7 from Nikkei 225, *http://markets.ft.com/markets/interactiveChart.asp;* Figure 4.8 from Nikkei 225, *http://markets.ft.com/markets/interactiveChart.asp;* Figure 5.1 from S&P 500, *http://markets.ft.com/markets/interactiveChart.asp;* Figure 5.2 from S&P 500, *http://markets.ft.com/markets/interactiveChart.asp;* Figure 5.3 from S&P 500, *http://markets.ft.com/markets/interactiveChart.asp;* Figure 6.1 from S&P 500, *http://markets.ft.com/markets/interactiveChart.asp;* Figure 6.2 from S&P 500, *http://markets.ft.com/markets/interactiveChart.asp;* Figure 6.3 from S&P 500, *http://markets.ft.com/markets/interactiveChart.asp;* Figure 6.4 from S&P 500, *http://markets.ft.com/markets/interactiveChart.asp;* Figure 6.5 from S&P 500, *http://markets.ft.com/markets/interactiveChart.asp;* Figure 6.6 from S&P 500, *http://markets.ft.com/markets/interactiveChart.asp;* Figure 7.1 from FTSE 100 *http://markets.ft.com/markets/interactiveChart.asp;* Figure 7.2 from FTSE 100 *http://markets.ft.com/markets/interactiveChart.asp;* Figure 7.4 from FTSE 100 *http://markets.ft.com/markets/interactiveChart.asp;* Figure 9.1 from FTSE 100 http://markets.ft.com/markets/interactiveChart.asp

In some instances we have been unable to trace the owners of copyright material, and we would appreciate any information that would enable us to do so.

Preface: what makes an exceptional trader

Investment is a fascinating subject that has intrigued many over the centuries. It amasses fortunes for some, loses millions for others. In today's fast-moving financial markets, more fortunes are made and lost than ever before, and in record time.

To be a savvy investor, you need the extra proven edge to ensure that your investments grow at the expense of uninformed investors. In order to make it in this game, you will need a statistical trading edge that has been proven to generate net abnormal returns in the long run. You will need a tool to gain this statistical trading edge and the tool is simply your very own mechanical trading system.

This book is a guide to a trader's journey in search of that 'ideal' algorithm trading system that gives you this statistical trading edge, one that can decipher market patterns and detect trends to generate net abnormal returns in the long run.

The Financial Times Guide to Technical Analysis is a trader's guidebook, written by a trader for traders – and you can become a successful one too. It is hoped that all traders will benefit from the book's content. Using the same concepts and principles as those used by financial institutions, the book places retail investors on level ground with institutional traders. It guides them to make abnormal returns with their own technical professional trading systems.

This book is about how you can be a smarter investor, one who grows capital in the stock and futures markets. It is about how you, the smart amateur investor, take control of your financial future in all the financial markets. This book will show you how to assess the markets technically and time your investment in a way that lets your capital grow while limiting your losses all the way.

You will see how some successful professionals make profits consistently with technical analysis techniques and formulas, and learn how to apply the concepts and principles that professional traders use. You will also be exposed to insider knowledge and concepts from behind the trading desks of financial institutions.

The Financial Times Guide to Technical Analysis consists of two parts. The first part – What do traders know? – is an introduction to technical analysis. This basic level introduction is written for investors who are new to technical analysis. It gives new traders an overview of the tools that are available in technical analysis and guidance on how to use them.

The second part – Trading with professional technical systems – concentrates on the strategies used in trading. This advanced level is written for serious investors who are willing to commit time, money and endurance to trade profitably. It analyses a particular trading system – BBZ – and related trading plans, strategies and risk control management. It gives instructions to traders on how to develop and optimise a trading system; and it shows how simple moving average and standard deviations can be used for model building.

Objectives

The purpose of compiling this book is to ensure that you gain a comprehensive understanding of the tools used by traders. Therefore, one of our objectives is to explore some simple trading techniques from a selection of technical analysis tools to design and build mechanical trading systems. The ultimate aim is to develop you, the reader, into a good trader.

My aim is that anyone who picks up this book will be able to apply the tools and techniques easily. This book condenses the most important investment principles of a full three-year undergraduate finance course into those relevant to the trading practitioner dealing in today's markets. You do not need to go through three years of a full-time finance course to become a professional trader, just start by reading this book.

Important points to remember

What marks an exceptional trader from an average trader is a proven statistical trading edge of producing positive net returns in the long run. An exceptional trader is not born with a natural gaming talent to time purchases and sales. Rather he or she is someone who is an extremely keen observer of market price patterns. The exceptional trader does his or her homework by researching the markets and backtesting a technical trading system. Anyone can be an exceptional trader if he or she dedicates and commits the time to study and practise technical analysis in the science of trading. This book aims to develop an exceptional trader – you.

The FT Guide to Technical Analysis provides the basic foundations of technical analysis and trading systems. It explains the concepts of technical indicators in the research, design and backtesting of a mechanical trading system. The book begins by looking at the behaviour of market prices and introduces technical analysis to these price patterns. The second part of the book is on trading and the trading systems that professional traders use. These cover the complete subject of technical analysis and trading at beginner and intermediate levels. No prior knowledge is required.

The book introduces insiders' concepts and principles on becoming a professional trader. The approach is of a mentor professional trader guiding a favourite apprentice in the fine science of trading with technical analysis. These insider concepts and principles are simple and effective and they can easily be learnt and applied.

Before investing in anything, at any time, home- and groundwork is a must. This book helps in guiding you through that basic, essential, background work. It is dedicated to showing you how to time the purchase and sale of financial instruments in a way that makes your capital grow in the long run. It aims to fill the gap between the shortcomings in further and higher financial education and the vast, complex markets that confront us all.

So, this book is for anyone who wants to do better in the financial markets, especially the stocks and futures markets. It is for those who want a greater understanding of the stock and futures markets, enabling them to manage their investments better by controlling their risks.

Why you need to know technical analysis to trade

Technical analysis is the study of price patterns to identify trading opportunities; it is about charting data and interpreting charts using technical tools and techniques. These techniques are instilled into formulas which are called mechanical trading systems in accordance with specific trading plans. Good trading plans encompass the estimations of traders' rewards and risks. Very good trading plans specify the strategies for entry and risk control management. Essentially, good trading plans are part of good money management.

Technical analysis, one of the most important investment subjects, is what every investor needs to learn before making any trading decisions, especially in regard to the timing of a purchase or sale of any financial asset. Every wise investor knows that each financial market has its own cycles, and making abnormal, exceptional profits is all about knowing and following the patterns of these seasons.

This book is all about guiding the average investor to use the right technical indicators to detect these timings in order to make exceptional profits. It is about how you can distinguish yourself from the crowd and make exceptional profits using not only the given tools in this book but also tools that you, yourself, have invented.

The Financial Times Guide to Technical Analysis will appeal to anyone interested in the stock and futures markets. It is a succinct professional trading guide for the individual serious investor, whether an amateur or someone with some knowledge of investment. It begins with a guided tour of the world of investing and gives practical advice on trading opportunities and the corresponding appropriate strategies using well-known and newly innovated technical analysis concepts.

How to use this book

The book is written in an easy to read technical traders' language, for anyone who wants to find the extra edge to trading. It begins with some traders' terms that you need to become familiar with to get a basic overview of this book's subject matter. (These terms are also covered in the glossary at the end of the book.)

You will notice that each chapter begins with two short sections:

- What topics are covered in this chapter?
- What are the objectives?

A brief background introduction sets the scene and the important points are then clearly laid out, followed by in-depth discussion and trading examples and exercises where necessary. The chapter's concepts are summed up in a chapter review for quick revision. Finally, in 'A Note to the trading apprentice' I list some of my observations, theories and trading experiences, often as a caution on where not to tread and when not to trade.

My main note to the trading apprentice – you – is that trading is not an art but a serious profession that can be learnt and applied profitably. Technical analysis is a quantitative science with proven functional theorems that every trader can use. You too can start trading for a living. If at the end of this book you can trade professionally, this guide will have achieved its objective.

It is my hope that after reading this book, you will trade the markets in a different way – a more professional way. It is your personal responsibility to learn trading as a profession and this book will help you towards this goal. I aim to show the way that professional traders play this game, so read this book with an open mind and follow each step carefully. One day soon, using the concepts that I have laid out here, you may be building better trading models than the ones in this book. When that day comes, this book will have achieved its purpose. I would be delighted to learn about and discuss your trading model with you if you email me at trading-forarealiving@lycos.com.

All the best in your trading.

Jacinta Chan

Neither the author nor the publisher can accept responsibility for any loss occasioned to any person who either acts or refrains from acting as a result of any statement in this book. Readers should note that the author is not recommending the purchase or sale of any particular financial security: references to companies are made for illustration.

Some traders' terms

Analysis

Fundamental analysis The study of economic information to forecast prices and to gauge if an asset is overvalued or undervalued. It is an analysis of current economic conditions to calculate the fair value and forecast the future price of an asset.

Technical analysis The study of price movements using past prices, volume and open interest to identify trading opportunities. It is an analysis of historical price data to identify price trends. Technical analysis includes a variety of techniques such as chart analysis, pattern recognition, seasonality and cycle analysis, and algorithm technical trading systems.

Chart analysis

Chart A graphical record of prices and volume, taken at regular intervals.

Close/closing price The last trade price for the period.

High The highest price traded for the period.

Low The lowest price traded for the period.

Open/opening price The first traded price for the period.

Open interest The number of futures contracts that have been opened and have not been closed. The amount of futures contracts that are still open and in existence.

Volume The number of contracts/shares traded for the period.

Technical indicators

Bands Lines constructed around a moving average that define relative high and low.

Bband Z-test statistics (BBZ) A technical trading system that uses as a default one standard deviation around a default 21-day moving average (to give a long signal above the one standard deviation band and a short signal below the one standard deviation band).

Absolute range breakout A technical trading system that indicates a buy signal when the close is above the high of the previous number of days and a sell signal when the close is below the low of the previous number of days.

Moving average (MA) The measure of the average price over the previous periods that is recomputed each succeeding period using the most recent data.

Moving average convergence and divergence (MACD) An indicator that uses the difference between a 12-day and a 26-day moving average to indicate a buy signal if the difference is more than the average difference of the previous nine days and a sell signal if the difference is less than the average difference of the previous nine days.

Optimised Bband Z-test statistics (OptBBZ) A technical trading system that uses optimised parameters for standard deviation and moving average (to give a long signal above the optimised standard deviation band and a short signal below the optimised standard deviation band).

Trading range terms

Trading range A price range in which trading has been confined for an extended period. Generally sideways in character.

Trading range system A trading system that tries to sell at the resistance and to buy at the support on the assumption that the market will pull back at the resistance and support levels.

Resistance An area on a chart above the current price where identifiable trading has occurred before. It is believed that investors who bought at those higher prices will become sellers when those prices are reached again, thus halting an advance.

Support An area where declines are halted and reversed. Support is often associated with perceived value.

Trading trend terms

Algorithm trading system A trading system with a set of trading rules that mathematically computes according to an algorithm (suitable to the prevailing market conditions) mechanically generated signals (long, short or out-of-market) indicating when to enter and when to exit, and executes the trades automatically. Algorithmic trading (or automated or algo, or black box or robo trading) is the computer program that executes trades according to an algorithm that is suitable to prevailing market conditions. The algorithm in the program is derived after intensive backtesting and optimisation. Algorithm trading programmes are popularly employed by professional model trading desks of large financial institutions.

Trend trading system A trading system with a set of trading rules that defines when to initiate a position early to capture the prevailing trend using a mechanically generated signal on the assumption that the trend will continue. Moving average and standard deviation are technical indicators used in trend trading systems.

Downtrend A state in which prices are steadily declining.

Uptrend A state in which prices are steadily increasing.

Tests

Backtest The process of testing using historical data.

Optimisation The process of finding the best performing parameter for a trading system.

Parameter A value assigned to a trading system to vary/optimise the timing of the signal.

Theories

Dow theory An observation (initially by Charles Dow) which states that:

The averages must confirm each other.

■ The averages discount everything.
■ The market has three movements.
■ The major trends have three phases.
■ Volume must confirm trend.
■ A trend continues until the signal reverses.

Elliott wave theory An observation (initiated by R. N. Elliott) which states that all market activities develop into well-ordered patterns consisting of five primary impulse waves followed by three correction waves.

Fractal geometry An observation (initially by Benoit Mandelbrot) which states that there are repeating patterns in nature including time series.

Random walk theory An observation (initially by Eugene Fama) which states that the history of the series cannot be used to predict the future in any meaningful way and that the future path of the price of a security is no more predictable than the path of a series of cumulated random numbers (Fama, 1965).

Trading terms

Fill Getting the order done.

Long The state of owning a security.

Short The state of being short a security. The act of selling before buying.

Rollover The closing of the front month's position and the opening of the next month's position.

Slippage cost The cost of the difference between the theoretical execution price and the actual price executed due to poor fill.

Volatility The tendency for prices to vary. Standard deviation and variance are measures of volatility.

Whipsaw A period of wrong signals that result in losses

What do traders know?

Introduction: the market technicians

Professional traders are market technicians who are financial experts in the practical science of trading. Today's market technicians usually use technical analysis to trade in the financial markets they specialise in. They use price charts and technical analysis tools to make trading decisions.

Before they trade, traders have trading plans. These plans are their special trading edge. Their trading edge charts the future of their trading experience to be that of net positive return. Therefore, their trading plans are usually based on historical patterns of statistical price returns. They plan their trading before they begin and they begin with research.

Strange as it may seem, many people who are trading in stocks and futures do not know what they are doing. They repeatedly lose money and they do not even know why. The most common reason is that they fail to cut their losses early and even after a loss has been cut they cannot even contemplate why they have lost.

This book is arranged in topics to cover everything that the trader needs to make it as a professional. Anyone can be a trader but only those who have undergone and passed professional technical training and are trading seriously can be a professional trader.

In the author's experience, the topics that are important in the science of trading have their foundations in technical analysis, which can be viewed as the cornerstone of professional trading.

The topics that are important in basic technical analysis are:

■ charts

■ classical reversal and continuation patterns

■ gaps

■ trends

■ moving averages

■ momentum

■ range breakouts

■ projection levels

■ risk and returns

■ the trading system.

This introduction defines the market technician who is a trader in terms of Dow theory and trading.

The learning objectives of this part are to guide you, step by step, to:

■ learn how to construct and read your own chart

■ identify reversal and continuation chart patterns

■ spot bubbles and gaps, and then follow the trend winners

■ construct common technical indicators like moving average and put them to use in your trading

■ identify the profit-making opportunities and the possible projection of how far the trend will carry

■ learn the basics of a trading system.

Firm foundations

The first foundations of technical analysis were laid by Charles Dow in a series of *Wall Street Journal* editorials in the late 1800s and early 1900s. Charles Dow, the editor, founder and part owner of the *Wall Street Journal* and the creator of the Dow Jones Index, penned his observations and analysis of the US stock market in a series of Review and Outlook editorials in the Journal. His observations and analysis were later called the Dow theory.

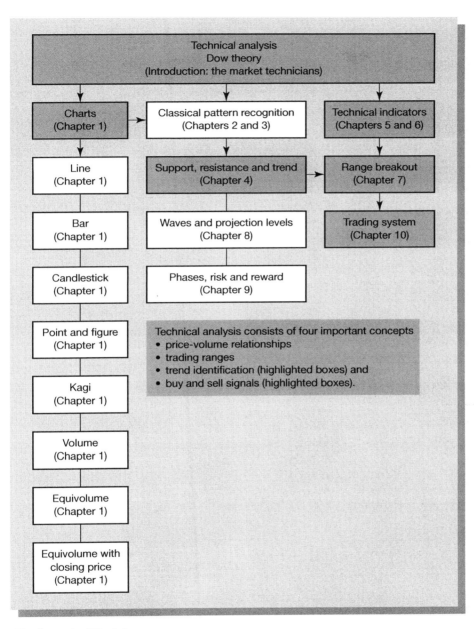

The layout of Part 1

Dow theory

Dow theory covers six basic tenets that form the foundations of technical analysis:

1   The averages (industrial and transportation) must confirm each other.
2   The averages discount everything.
3   The market has three movements.
4   The major trends have three phases.
5   Volume must confirm trend.
6   A trend continues until the signal reverses.

The market's three movements are:

1   primary movements (lasting for years)
2   secondary correction movements (lasting for months) and
3   daily fluctuations.

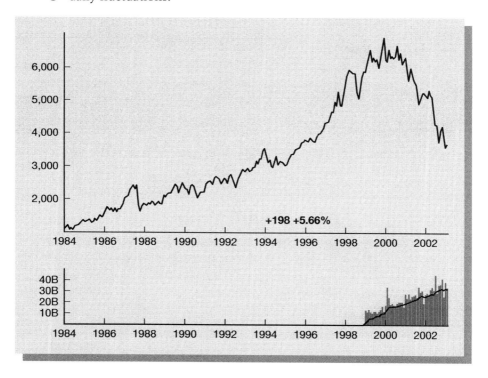

Chart showing accumulation, uptrend, excess, distribution, downtrend and despair

Source: From FTSE 100, http://markets.ft.com/markets/interactiveChart.asp

In a bull primary movement, the three phases are:

1 accumulation

2 big up move (uptrend) and

3 excess.

In a bear primary movement, the three phases are:

1 distribution

2 big down move (downtrend) and

3 despair.

Usually the beginning of the uptrend or downtrend is confirmed by a rising volume. This trend continues until the signal shows reversal and the signal can be obtained from the averages.

Traders' terms – technical analysis

Technical analysis basically consists of four important concepts.

1 price–volume relationships

2 trading ranges

3 trend identification and

4 buy and sell signals.

Rising volumes with rising prices confirm an uptrend while rising volumes with falling prices confirm a downtrend. The market is said to be range trading if it trades between support and resistance. Scalpers and day traders looking for very short-term profits buy at points where they perceive there is support and sell where there is resistance. However, trend traders look for confirmation of a downtrend on the breaking support level to sell and an uptrend on the breaking resistance level to buy.

Basically, all these concepts apply in trading. These concepts take the forms of different technical indicators such as moving averages. This book is organised to cover these concepts in the order price–volume relationships, trading ranges, trend identification and mechanical trading signals.

Review

The first foundations of technical analysis were laid by Charles Dow about a century ago. They were later known as Dow theory and cover six basic tenets:

1 The averages must confirm each other.

2 The averages discount everything.

3 The market has three movements.

4 The major trends have three phases.

5 Volume must confirm trend.

6 A trend continues until the signal reverses.

The market's three movements are primary movements, secondary correction movements and daily fluctuations. In a bull primary movement, the three phases are accumulation, big uptrend and excess. In a bear primary movement, the three phases are distribution, big downtrend and despair.

Technical analysis consists of four important concepts, price–volume relationships, trading ranges, trend identification and trading signals.

A NOTE TO THE TRADING APPRENTICE

Plan your trades and trade your plan

The problem with most people is that they start to trade before they are mentally prepared. They trade without any good technical foundation and without any plans. They trade without even knowing the different phases of the market or the relationship between present and past price behaviours.

They use their gut feelings and emotions when they could use simple trading plans. Professional traders, on the other hand, trade with their own plans and trading systems, and without emotion. Professional traders are defined as traders who make profit consistently as a profession.

This book seeks to address this problem by guiding the beginner trader through the process of charting, reading charts with technical indicators and writing trading plans according to projected returns against expected risks. This book is about designing and developing your own trading system and provides the reader with a time-tested plan for trading. If used with discipline, it is a short cut to becoming a professional trader because the tools and techniques are clearly spelt out in the different chapters.

You do not have to learn from your own mistakes! In trading, this is too costly. Learn from others' mistakes by doing your own thorough research before committing to your first trade. By reading this book, the theoretical research has been done for you. After this, you should be ready to start your practical training – by trading.

You must have a plan before you even think of trying to trade for a living. This book is specifically written to help you with a plan to start trading for a living. To build the plan, we must first have a firm foundation of knowledge and skill.

The first step is to know the market and Chapter 1 shows how you can do this by constructing your own chart.

1

Know the market: how to read and construct charts

What topics are covered in this chapter?

Technical analysis is defined as the in-depth study of the behaviour of market prices on charts and it begins with the different types of chart:

- line
- bar
- candlestick
- point and figure
- kagi
- volume
- equivolume
- equivolume with closing price

What are the objectives?

- To know how to construct line, bar and candlestick charts.
- To read volume charts and understand the relationship between price and volume.
- To know what point-and-figure, kagi and equivolume charts are.
- To read and interpret your own chart for your own trading purposes.
- To understand what technical analysis is all about and the basic principles underlying the study of technical analysis.

Introduction

The chart is the most basic and important tool of technical analysis. Charting is important in order to understand the behaviour of market prices. When you can chart your own graph of historical prices, you can also project the probabilities of your trading strategies being profitable in the long run. This chapter will show you how to chart prices and volume in a graph that you can use for your own trading.

Definitions of technical analysis

Technical analysis is the study of historical price data to identify price trends and forecast price movements. It is the analysis of price activities or patterns to identify trading opportunities. As an approach to financial investment, technical analysis is based on the general principle that history tends to repeat itself.

Technical analysis states that all information is discounted in the price, that the result of such information causes the price to trend, and that price patterns tend to repeat. This implies that the recurring price patterns can provide signs to probable future price movements and trends. Thus, the way to trade equity and commodity is to identify patterns and signals that indicate the beginning of new trends.

Technical analysis involves price and sometimes volume study and is different from fundamental analysis. Fundamental analysis involves the study of economic information to forecast prices and to gauge if an asset is overvalued or undervalued. Fundamental analysis looks in depth at the financial conditions and operating results of a specific company and the underlying behavior of its common stock. The value of a stock is established by analysing the fundamental information associated with the company such as accounting, competition and management.

Generally, fundamental analysis evaluates the economic condition of the country it operates in as well as the international economy, the industry, the factors affecting the industry and finally the company itself to determine the intrinsic value of the share. If the intrinsic value is higher than the market price, a buy recommendation will be issued by the research analyst. Similarly, if the intrinsic value is lower than the market price, a sell recommendation will be issued.

However, most stocks cannot be accurately valued due to inadequate representation of the facts and values attached to the management and the future of the company, the industry and the economy at large. The fundamental factors are overshadowed by the supply and demand of the stock. This supply and demand will result in the prevailing market price.

Technical analysis can be said to focus on the resulting trend and not on the reason for the market trend, whereas fundamental analysis is concerned with the economic and specific reasons for the price increase or decrease.

The underlying basis for technical analysis is that the price not only reflects all the information about that asset but also reflects the opinion of all market participants regarding that information. The information and market opinion reflected by the prices will result in recurring price patterns that provide clues to future price movements, range trading or trend trading. Generally, traditional classical technical analysis deals with price patterns' recognition of possible supports and resistances whereas today's contemporary technical analysis is more concerned with scientific measures of quantitative results to identify trends.

Classical technical analysis can be defined as the art of recognising price behaviours in the historical patterns that they form and forecasting patterns they might form. Classical technical analysis concentrates more on range trading between support and resistance. Therefore, it is more predictive in nature.

Contemporary technical analysis believes that there is systematic statistical dependency in asset returns. It concentrates more on trend trading and therefore is more reactive to the market.

By analysing historical price patterns, technical analysts look for price behaviours that suggest the possible initiation, conclusion or continuation of trends. Therefore, technical analysis makes price forecasts based on past data, looking for patterns and applying trading rules to charts to assess ranges, support levels, resistance levels and trends. From these, market technicians develop buy and sell signals.

A trading system built on technical analysis will give appropriate buy and sell signals based on pattern recognition with the objective of making the maximum amount of money, at minimum risk.

Charting

As technical analysis is a study of price activities or price patterns, it is necessary to plot the historical price data on a chart. A chart provides a concise price history; essential information for the trader.

A chart is used as a timing tool for the trader on when to enter the market and when to exit on taking profit or cutting loss, as in the case of risk management. A chart provides the trader with an idea of the market's expected return and volatility (risk). From the chart and technical indicators such as Bollinger bands, it can be observed that when the deviations are wider, the expected returns are much larger. This is in line with finance theory taught in further education that the higher the risk, the higher the expected return.

Therefore, a good understanding of charting is important and essential for trading profitably.

Constructing your own chart

To construct a chart you need to plot the closing price and some other prices, such as opening price, period high and period low as well as the volume for the period. In constructing a futures chart, the open interest for outstanding contracts can be included.

DEFINITIONS OF PRICE, VOLUME AND OPEN INTEREST

Open – The first trade for the period (e.g. the first traded price of the day).

High – The highest price traded for the period (e.g. the highest traded price of the day).

Low – The lowest price traded for the period (e.g. the lowest traded price of the day).

Close – The last trade for the period (e.g. the last traded price of the day).

Volume – The number of contracts traded during the period (e.g. the number of contracts traded for the day).

Open interest – The number of outstanding contracts (i.e. those contracts that have not been closed or settled).

Bid – The price that a buyer is willing to pay for a contract.

Ask – The price that a seller is willing to receive for a contract.

A chart can incorporate the open, high, low, close, volume and open interest. These are the factors that technical analysts use to determine if the market is in range trading or in trend trading. Different tools and techniques will be required in a range trading market as opposed to a trend trading market.

To study the price patterns, a chart can be constructed with the price levels on the vertical axis and time on the horizontal axis. Volume can be charted at the bottom of the graph.

Prices are depicted on charts. The price chart is the most basic technical analysis tool. A chart is a record, in graphic form, of market information, taken at regular intervals. The intervals or periodity may be by tick, minute, hour, day, week, month or quarter depending on the timeframe (short-term, medium-term or long-term) that the investor is interested in. Usually, the short-term timeframe is used for quicker entries and exits while the long-term timeframe is used to confirm entries and exits.

There are many types of chart but the most popular ones can be categorised as:

▦ line chart

▦ bar chart

▦ candlestick chart

▦ point and figure chart

▦ kagi chart

▦ volume chart

▦ equivolume chart

▦ equivolume chart with closing prices.

To see and draw some of these charts, we have included a series of exercises, as below. These exercises are instruction sessions on how to draw charts using http://markets.ft.com/markets/interactiveChart.asp. They are aimed at the novice trader who wants to try everything hands on to gain familiarity with the techniques and skills of drawing charts and constructing technical indicators. As we go, we will read and interpret the charts in the main text.

Exercise

1 Log on to http://markets.ft.com/markets/interactiveChart.asp

2 Type and select FTSE 100 Index. You should see a preconstructed line chart with a marker on the date.

3 Moving the marker, you will see the closing price, opening price, high price, low price and volume for each day.

Line chart

A line chart involves plotting and joining the **close** of each period. A line chart of daily closing prices is constructed in Figure 1.1.

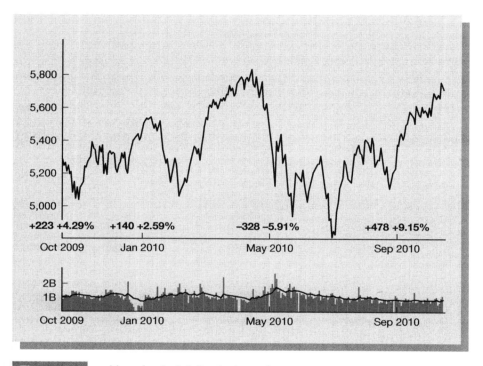

Figure 1.1   Line chart of daily closing prices
Source: From FTSE 100, http://markets.ft.com/markets/interactiveChart.asp

A line chart gives only limited information about the day's closing price. For more information on the day's activities, an open, high, low, close chart can be constructed. A bar chart can depict open, high, low and close.

Bar (OHLC) chart

A bar (OHLC) chart (see Figure 1.2) involves plotting:

▥ **high** and **low** as a vertical line with the top tip of the vertical line being the period's high and the bottom tip being the period's low

▨ **open** as a small horizontal line to the left of the vertical line and

▨ **close** as a small horizontal line to the right of the vertical line.

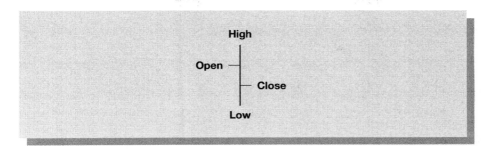

Figure 1.2   **A bar chart**

Example

On 15/10/2010, for the FTSE 100:

Open = 5,727.21

High = 5,743.92

Low = 5,665.95

Close = 5,703.37.

The bar chart or OHLC chart can be depicted as shown here:

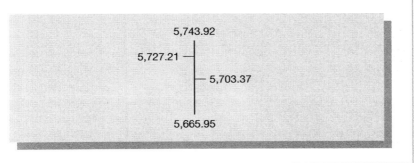

Exercise

In http://markets.ft.com/markets/interactiveChart.asp this bar chart is called OHLC.

1 Change 'Chart Style' to 'OHLC'.

2 A daily bar chart is as shown in Figure 1.3.

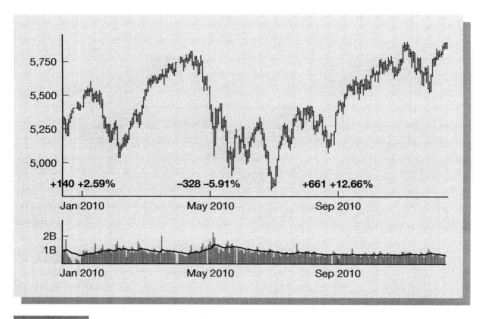

Figure 1.3   **A bar chart of daily prices**

Source: From FTSE 100, http://markets.ft.com/markets/interactiveChart.asp

Now, we are starting to see more information. To put it more graphically and to see if the close at the end of the day is higher than the open, or vice versa, we can try a candlestick chart.

Candlestick chart

A candlestick chart (see Figure 1.4) involves plotting:

▨ The body – a rectangular box with the top and bottom representing the period's **open** and **close** or vice versa. It is not filled or white if the period's close is higher than the period's open. It is filled or black if the period's close is lower than the period's open.

▨ The top shadow – a vertical line that extends from the top of the rectangular box representing the period's **high**.

▨ The bottom shadow – a vertical line that extends from the bottom of the rectangular box representing the period's **low**.

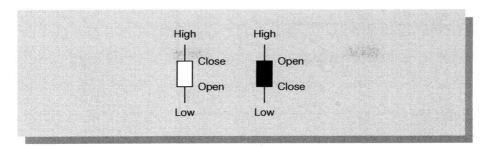

Figure 1.4 **A candlestick chart**

On 15/10/2010, for the FTSE 100:

Open = 5,727.21
High = 5,743.92
Low = 5,665.95
Close = 5,703.37.

The candlestick chart can be depicted as shown here:

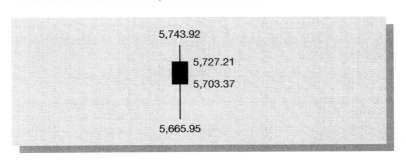

1 In http://markets.ft.com/markets/interactiveChart.asp change 'Chart Style' to 'Candle'.

2 A daily candlestick chart is as shown in Figure 1.5.

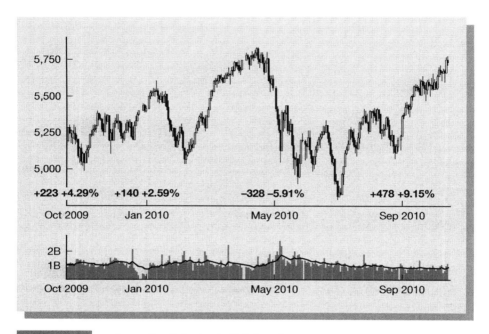

Figure 1.5   A candlestick chart of daily prices

Source: From FTSE 100, http://markets.ft.com/markets/interactiveChart.asp

Originating in Japan, candlestick charts are used to identify price patterns.

A long white candlestick is a bullish formation where there is a wide trading range where the open is near the low and the close is near the high (see Figure 1.6A). A long black candlestick is a bearish formation where there is a wide trading range where the open is near the high and the close is near the low (see Figure 1.6B).

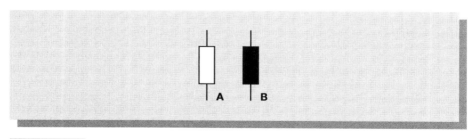

Figure 1.6   A long white candlestick (A) and a long black candlestick (B)

Candlestick reversal signs

Doji is a reversal sign where the open is the same as the close. It is bullish in a downtrend and bearish in an uptrend (see Figure 1.7A).

Bullish engulfing is bullish sign in a downtrend when a big white shadowless candlestick engulfs a small black shadowless candlestick (see Figure 1.7B).

Bearish engulfing is a bearish sign in an uptrend when a big black shadowless candlestick engulfs a small white shadowless candlestick (see Figure 1.7C).

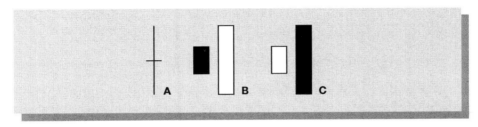

Figure 1.7   **Candlestick reversal signs**

Point and figure chart

Point and figure was used by floor traders who carried small paper notebooks and pens in their trading vest jackets. It is a convenient way to jot down every tick movement of the prices and refer to them. Floor traders use these as their charts and read from them.

A point and figure chart involves plotting:

▦ a series of Xs to indicate advancing prices and

▦ a series of Os to indicate declining prices.

A point and figure chart does not involve a time scale for the horizontal axis. A point and figure chart moves to the next column of price activity only if prices have reversed direction by a predetermined amount known as the reversal number.

Exercise

1 In http://markets.ft.com/markets/tearsheets/performance.asp, click on 'Historic Prices'.

2 Follow the instructions on the website (shade the data you wish, right-click and then select copy).

3 Paste the copied data onto a worksheet (highlight a cell, right-click, select Paste Special and then choose text or HTML format).

4 Using only the closing prices, you may start to draw an X for every up day and an O for every down day.

5 Use the next column to show a reversal after three consecutive days of the opposite sign. For example, if prices are advancing, we need three consecutive downdays to draw the three Os in the next column.

Note that a point and figure chart is usually used for tick charting and not daily charting. This exercise is conducted to show that historical prices can be extracted from http://markets.ft.com and that they can be used in a spreadsheet to draw point and figure charts or to calculate any technical indicator for any trading system.

A point and figure chart is shown in Figure 1.8.

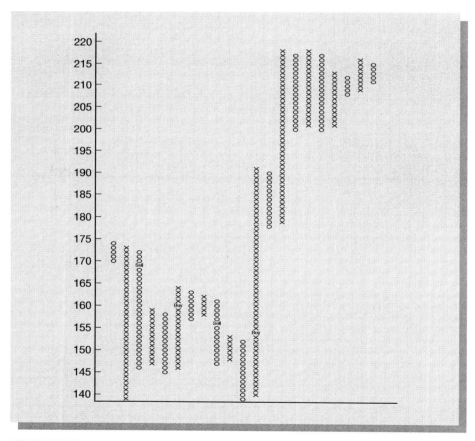

Figure 1.8   Point and figure chart of Apple daily closing prices

Source: Data of AAPL:NSQ from 18/6/2010 to 15/12/2010 from
http://markets.ft.com/tearsheets/performance.asp?s=AAPL:NSQ

As a rough guide, the buy signal appears after the price passes above the previous X on the way up and the sell signal appears after the price passes below the previous O on the way down.

In the Apple stock listed on the Nasdaq example shown in Figure 1.8, the buy signal appeared on 22/7/2010 at 260 and the sell signal appeared on 11/8/2010 at 256. The next buy signal appeared on 254 and as of 15/12/2010 the long signal is still on with the price at 320 (a paper gain of 66).

However, note that different traders use point and figure differently. Some traders wait for pullback to enter a new position. The drawback of this technique is that when prices start to break out, sometimes they do not retrace back.

Some traders look for price patterns in the point and figure chart before entering a position. We are going to discuss price patterns in Chapter 2.

Kagi chart

A kagi chart involves plotting:

- blue coloured lines when the current price moves higher than the most recent previous high
- red coloured lines when the current price moves lower than the most recent previous low.

A kagi chart does not involve a time scale for the horizontal axis. It moves to the next column of price activity only if prices have reversed direction by a predetermined amount known as the reversal number.

The kagi chart is similar to a point and figure chart except that it uses red for a short position and blue for a long position.

Exercise

1 In http://markets.ft.com/markets/tearsheets/performance.asp, click on 'Historic Prices'.

2 Follow the instructions in the spreadsheet.

3 Paste the copied data onto a worksheet.

4 Using only the closing prices, you can start to colour blue for every up day and red for every down day.

5 Use the next column to show a reversal after three consecutive days of the opposite sign. For example, if prices are advancing, we need three consecutive downdays to colour the three red boxes on the next column.

Note that kagi charts are usually used for tick charting and not daily charting. This exercise is conducted to show that historical prices can be extracted from http://markets.ft.com and that they can be used in the spreadsheet to draw kagi or to calculate any technical indicator for any trading system.

A kagi chart is shown in Figure 1.9.

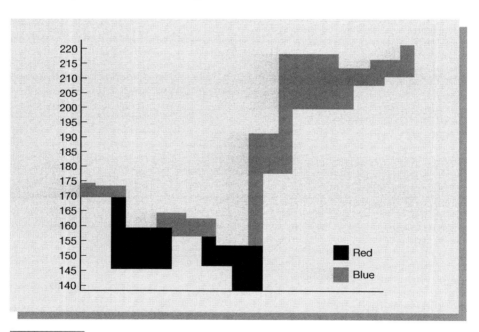

Figure 1.9   A kagi chart of Apple daily closing prices

Source: Data of AAPL:NSQ from 18/6/2010 to 15/12/2010 from
http://markets.ft.com/tearsheets/performance.asp?s=AAPL:NSQ

As a rough guide, the buy signal appears after the price passes above the previous high and the sell signal appears after the price passes below the previous low.

In the Apple stock listed in the Nasdaq example above, the buy signal appeared on 22/7/2010 at 260 and the sell signal appeared on 11/8/2010 at 256. The next buy signal appeared at 254 and as of 15/12/2010 the long signal is still on with the price at 320 (a paper gain of 66).

Note that the long position (blue) and the short position (red) are clearer in kagi than in point and figure. Also note that some traders use a three tops breakup before they enter a long position and a three bottoms breakdown before they enter a short position.

Now that you have constructed price charts, we can proceed to try to read these charts with a volume indicator.

Volume chart

A volume chart involves plotting the number of contracts traded as bars in a graph at the bottom of the previous chart(s). This is to show the relationship between price movements and volume traded:

▦ Increasing volume on rising prices is a bullish signal.

▦ Increasing volume on declining prices is a bearish signal.

▦ Decreasing volume on rising prices is a signal that a reversal is likely.

▦ Decreasing volume on declining prices is a signal that a reversal is likely.

A price and volume chart is shown in Figure 1.10.

Equivolume chart

Harold Gartley (better known as H. M. Gartley) in *Profits in the Stock Market* (1935) integrated volume into price charts. In *Profits in the Stock Market* (1935), Edward S. Quinn, writes in his article, 'The Economic Principles Employed in the Use and Interpretation of Trendographs', that in a standard Trendograph chart, the upper rectangles coordinate daily price ranges vertically and volume horizontally. Richard Arms discusses equivolume charts in *Profits in Volume: Equivolume Charting* (1998). All these contributed to the theory of equivolume charts.

An equivolume chart involves plotting equivolume bars (see Figure 1.11):

■ The height of each equivolume bar represents the **high** and **low** traded for the period.

■ The width of each equivolume bar represents the **volume** traded for the period.

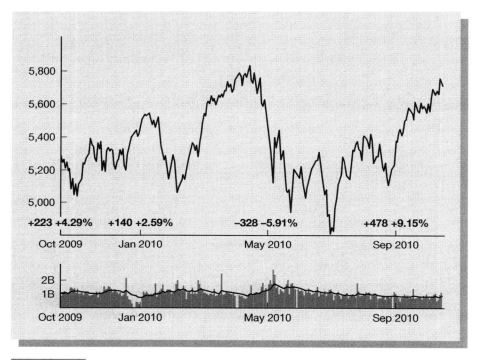

Figure 1.10   A volume chart with daily closing prices

Source: From FTSE 100, http://markets.ft.com/markets/interactiveChart.asp

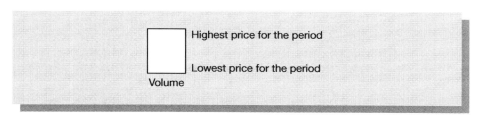

Figure 1.11   An equivolume bar

The shapes of these equivolume bars are used to show the commitment of buyers or sellers:

▦ A **narrow shape** denotes little commitment from buyers and sellers and therefore price movements are relatively easy (see Figure 1.12A).

▦ A **square shape** denotes some commitment from buyers and sellers and therefore price movements are relatively difficult (see Figure 1.12B).

▦ An **oversquare shape** denotes strong commitment from buyers and sellers. This can be a strong sign of reversal after a strong trend (see Figure 1.12C).

▦ A **power shape** denotes stronger commitment from either buyers or sellers and therefore price movements are in the favour and direction of the stronger party. It can serve as confirmation of breakout (see Figure 1.12D).

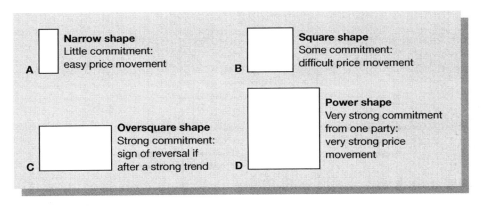

Figure 1.12   Equivolume bar shapes

An equivolume chart of daily prices and volume is shown in Figure 1.13.

It was a square shaped day on 13/10/2010, followed by a narrow shaped day on 14/10/2010, denoting little volume and narrow range, indicating that price movement would be easy. When buyers came in with volume on 15/10/2010, prices rose from a low of 305 to a high of 315 in a power shaped day. The following trading day,18/10/2010 was an oversquare shaped day denoting sellers with volume to match the buyers. This signalled a possible reversal. On 19/10/2010, prices fell from a high of 313 to a low of 300 on huge volume aggressive sellers in a power shaped day.

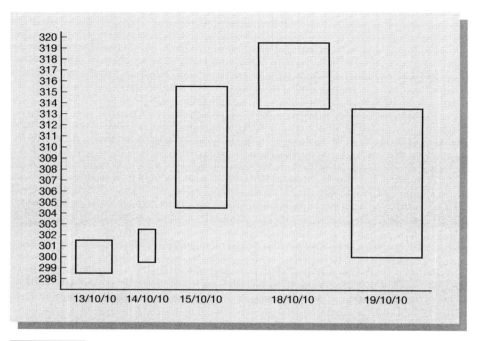

Figure 1.13   Equivolume chart of Apple daily closing prices

Source: Data of AAPL:NSQ from 18/6/2010 to 15/12/2010 from
http://markets.ft.com/tearsheets/performance.asp?s=AAPL:NSQ

Equivolume chart with closing prices

An equivolume chart with closing prices involves plotting a horizontal stroke as each closing price in the equivolume bar:

▓ If the closing price is higher than the previous closing price, the bar will be coloured blue and the area below the closing price will be coloured a deeper blue.

▓ If the closing price is lower than the previous closing price, the bar will be coloured red and the area above the closing price will be coloured a deeper red.

The position of the closing price in relation to the day's range indicates whether buyers or sellers have control. In an uptrend, if the closing price is nearer to the highest price for the period, buyers have control (see Figure 1.14).

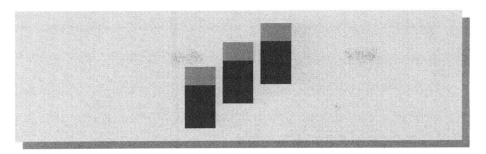

Figure 1.14   **Strong uptrend in equivolume chart with rising closing prices**

In a downtrend, if the closing price is nearer to the lowest price for the period, sellers have control (see Figure 1.15).

Figure 1.15   **Strong downtrend in equivolume chart with falling closing prices**

An example is shown in Figure 1.16.

Example

If you look at Figure 1.16 you will note that on 13/10/2010 it was a square shaped day with the closing price nearer the top, indicating that buyers have control. This is followed by a narrow shaped day on 14/10/2010, with the closing price at the top, indicating that buyers are more aggressive. When buyers came in with volume on 15/10/2010, prices rose from a low of 305 to a high of 315 in a power shaped day, pushing the price to close near the high at 314. The following trading day, 18/10/2010, was an oversquared day denoting sellers with volume to match the buyers. This signalled a possible reversal. On 19/10/2010, prices fell from a high of 313 to a low of 300 on huge volume sellers in a power shaped day.

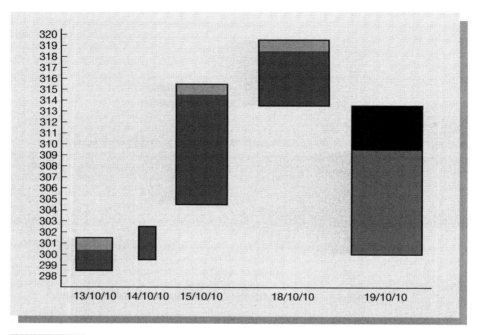

Figure 1.16   Equivolume with closing price chart of Apple daily closing prices

Source: Data of AAPL:NSQ from 18/6/2010 to 15/12/2010 from
http://markets.ft.com/tearsheets/performance.asp?s=AAPL:NSQ

Note that equivolume with closing price displays the strength of the buyers (or sellers) more clearly by showing how close the closing price is to the period's high (or low).

Chapter review

▪ Charts provide concise price history, which gives the trader some expectations of the return and volatility involved.

▪ Charts can be used as timing tools for trade entry and exit.

▪ Popular price chart types are the line chart, bar chart and candlestick chart.

▪ Besides price charts, there are also volume charts and equivolume charts which combine volume with price movements to decipher bullish or bearish price patterns.

▪ Increasing volumes on rising prices is a bullish sign and increasing volumes on falling prices a bearish sign.

A NOTE TO THE TRADING APPRENTICE

You must read your own chart

If you do not want to be misled by the crowd, you must read your own chart: no one can read it for you. You need to read your own chart to be able to calculate the probability of the profitability of your trades. Your own chart gives you a slight edge above those who do not read charts or rely on so-called experts who tell them what the 'experts' want them to believe.

By now, you should understand why you must never buy on a tip except when it is confirmed by an accumulation phase, followed by rising volume in an uptrend. Otherwise, in most cases, the tip may be a deliberate attempt to ramp the shares up for those who have bought at much lower prices and are looking for buyers to change hands at the higher prices.

Trust your charts but trade accordingly. This means that you should initiate a position on identification of a new trend, but always remember that half the time your entry will be wrong.

This is a probability game and the probability is always only 50% that the market will move in the direction of your trade. If the market moves against you, cut your loss quickly.

If the market moves in your favour, let the trend run its course. If there is a 50% chance of small losses and a 50% chance of huge gains the net trading experience will be large profits in the long run.

You must initiate a trade on identification of a new trend. Other than losses, the trader's greatest regret is missing a huge profit opportunity. If missed it will be very hard for him or her to recoup the small losses that have accumulated.

In reality, there is no expert chart reader; the art of pattern recognition is subjective. However, after the event, certain price patterns can be seen in terms of bullish or bearish signals. In the next chapter, we will go through what the chartists term a reversal or continuation of bullish and bearish signals.

2

History has a habit of repeating itself

What topics are covered in this chapter?

Reversal patterns are various types of exhaustion patterns derived from the prevailing trend and initiation of a new trend in the opposite direction. They include:

- head and shoulders
- tops and bottoms
- rounded top and rounded bottom
- V spike top and V spike bottom
- wedge reversal

Continuation patterns are various types of congestion phase that occur within long-term trends:

- triangles
- pennant
- flag
- rectangle

What are the objectives?

The objectives of pattern recognition are manifold:

- To know what the old school classical chartists are doing.
- To estimate the projection levels for repeating patterns.

Introduction

Classical technical analysis is about using charts to recognise price patterns. Price patterns have been observed to repeat over the past century. They are so remarkably typical that the term 'classical' is used. There are many similar patterns that can be recognised and grouped accordingly into reversal patterns or continuation patterns.

Reversal patterns

Head and shoulders

A head and shoulders is a bearish formation (see Figure 2.1). A head and shoulders top is formed when:

- at the left shoulder, the market rallies and then declines back to the neckline
- at the head, the market rallies to a higher level and then declines back to the neckline and
- at the right shoulder, the market rallies to a level lower than the head and then declines back to the neckline.

A head and shoulders top is formed before moving into a major downtrend when the price breaks below the neckline. It is only then that the sell signal emerges. The neckline is drawn by connecting the troughs between the two shoulders. Considerably lower prices are indicated when the market falls from the right shoulder to penetrate the neckline.

Exercise

1 Log on to: http://markets.ft.com/markets/interactiveChart.asp
2 Select Nikkei Index and you should see a preconstructed line chart.
3 Click on 'Trend Lines' at the bottom of the chart.
4 Click at the bottom of the left shoulder and then drag to the bottom of the right shoulder to form the neckline.
5 Extend the neckline to the left and to the right.

Figure 2.1 shows a head and shoulders formation.

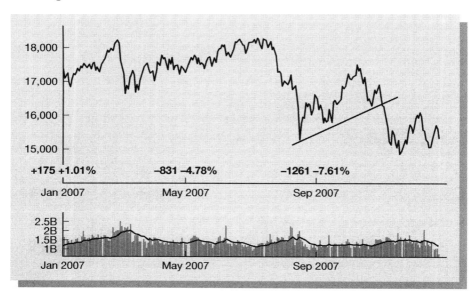

Figure 2.1   **A head and shoulders formation**

Source: From Nikkei 225, http://markets.ft.com/markets/interactiveChart.asp

An inverse head and shoulders is a bullish formation and is formed when:

▨ at the left shoulder, the market declines and then rallies back to the neckline

▨ at the head, the market declines to a lower level and then rallies back to the neckline and

▨ at the right shoulder, the market declines to a higher level than the inverse head and then rallies back to the neckline.

An inverse head and shoulders is formed before moving into a major uptrend when it breaks above the neckline. It is only then that the buy signal emerges. The neckline is drawn by connecting the peaks between the two shoulders. Considerably higher prices are indicated when the market rallies from the right shoulder to penetrate the neckline. (See Figure 2.2.)

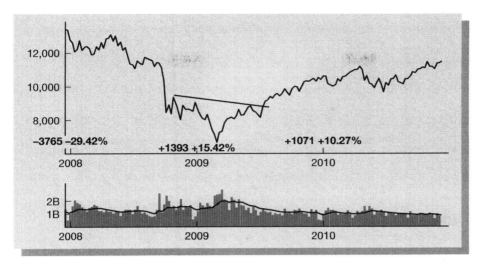

Figure 2.2   An inverse head and shoulders formation

Source: From DJIA, http://markets.ft.com/markets/interactiveChart.asp

Tops and bottoms

In classical technical analysis, it is common to identify peaks (tops) and troughs (bottoms) in price movements since these are traditional sell signals and buy signals respectively. The peaks are tops or areas where the selling pressure begins to drive prices down after an increase while the troughs are bottoms where the buying pressure begins to drive prices up after a decrease.

A double/triple top is a bearish formation. A double/triple top occurs when two/three successive highs reach approximately the same point. A double/triple top is considered to be formed when the fall from the second/third top moves down past the lowest trough between the two/three tops. It is only then the sell signal emerges. (See Figure 2.3.)

A double/triple bottom is a bullish formation. A double/triple bottom occurs when two/three successive lows reach approximately the same point. A double/triple bottom is considered to be formed when the rise from the second/third bottom moves down past the highest peak between the two/three tops. It is only then the buy signal emerges. (See Figure 2.4.)

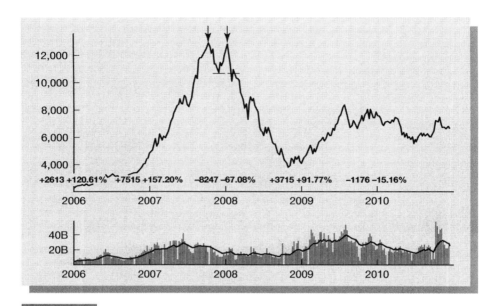

Figure 2.3   Double tops

Source: From SSE, http://markets.ft.com/markets/interactiveChart.asp

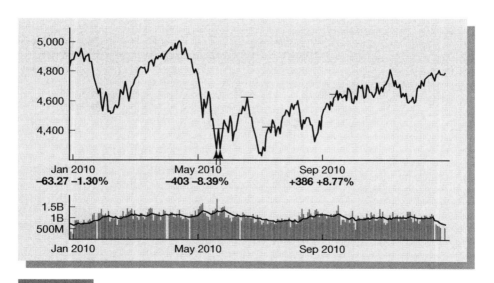

Figure 2.4   Double bottoms

Source: From ASX 200, http://markets.ft.com/markets/interactiveChart.asp

Rounded bottoms and tops

A rounded top is formed on the top of the price series with a convex curve under the highs. It signals a gradual change in the market where the initial buying pressure eases to be replaced by selling pressure. (See Figure 2.5.)

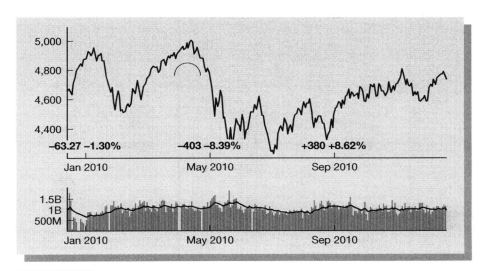

Figure 2.5   Rounded top

Source: From ASX200, http://markets.ft.com/markets/interactiveChart.asp

A saucer is formed as a round bottom with a concave curve under the lows. It signals a gradual change in the market where the initial selling pressure eases to be replaced by buying pressure. (See Figure 2.6.)

V spike top and bottom

A V spike top is a bearish formation after an extended uptrend where the unusual spike high day is above the highs on the preceding and succeeding days. Usually, the close on the spike high day is nearer to the low of the day. (See Figure 2.7.)

A V spike bottom is a bullish formation after an extended downtrend where the unusual spike low day is below the lows on the preceding and succeeding days. Usually, the close on the spike low day is nearer to the high of the day. (See Figure 2.8.)

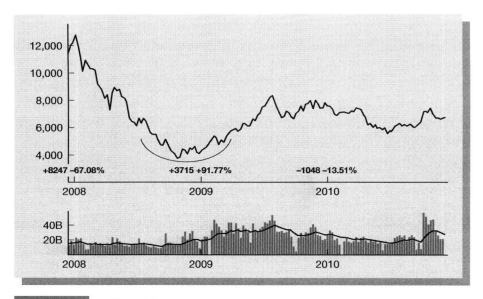

Figure 2.6   Round bottom

Source: From ASX, http://markets.ft.com/markets/interactiveChart.asp

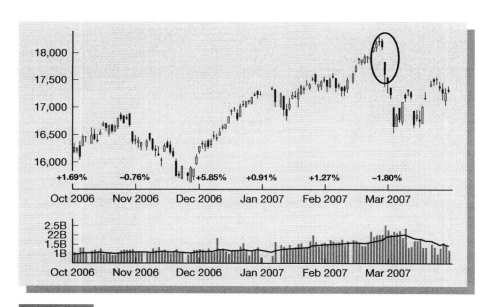

Figure 2.7   A V spike top

Source: From Nikkei 225, http://markets.ft.com/markets/interactiveChart.asp

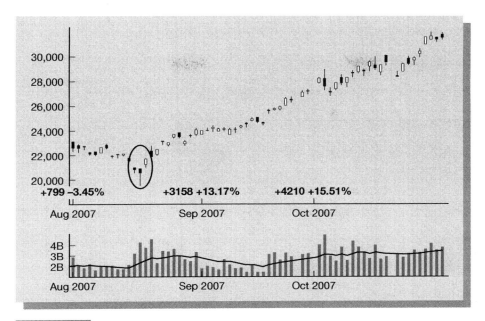

Figure 2.8   A V spike bottom
Source: From Hang Seng, http://markets.ft.com/markets/interactiveChart.asp

Wedge reversals

Wedge reversal formations are found at the bottom or the top of the trend. A wedge reversal formation must be followed by a breakout of the resistance or support line in the opposite direction to the prevailing trend.

A falling wedge is a bullish formation that is found at the bottom of the downtrend, when the prices converge in a downward sloping cone, followed immediately by a breakout of the resistance line into a new uptrend. (See Figure 2.9.)

A rising wedge is a bearish formation that is found at the top of the uptrend, when the prices converge in an upward sloping cone, followed immediately by a breakout of the support line into a downtrend. (See Figure 2.10.)

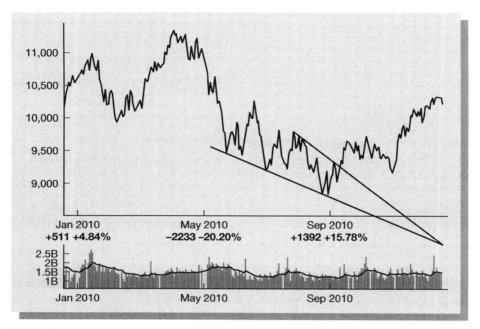

Figure 2.9   A falling wedge

Source: From Nikkei 225, http://markets.ft.com/markets/interactiveChart.asp

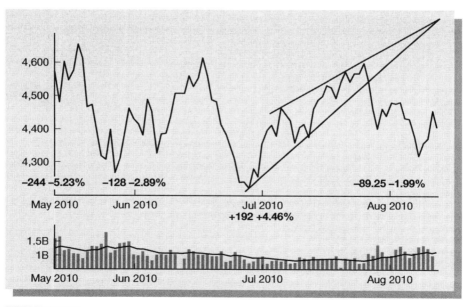

Figure 2.10   A rising wedge

Source: From ASX200, http://markets.ft.com/markets/interactiveChart.asp

Continuation patterns

Triangles

There are three types of triangle:

▧ symmetrical

▧ ascending

▧ descending.

A symmetrical triangle is usually followed by a continuation of the trend that preceded it (see Figure 2.11).

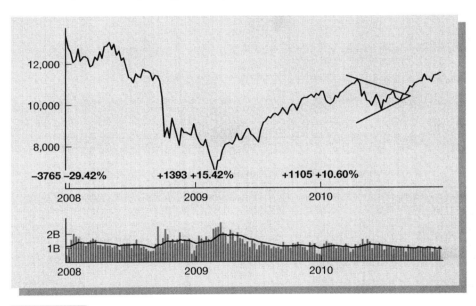

Figure 2.11   **A symmetrical triangle**

Source: From DJIA, http://markets.ft.com/markets/interactiveChart.asp

An ascending triangle is usually followed by a continuation of an uptrend except for the case of triangle breakdown. Then a downtrend is expected to follow (see Figure 2.12).

A descending triangle is usually followed by a continuation of a downtrend except for the case of a triangle breakup. Then an uptrend is expected to follow (see Figure 2.13).

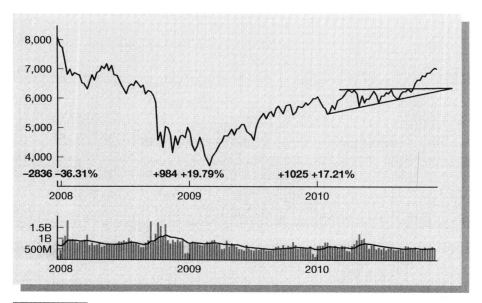

Figure 2.12   An ascending triangle

Source: From DAX, http://markets.ft.com/markets/interactiveChart.asp

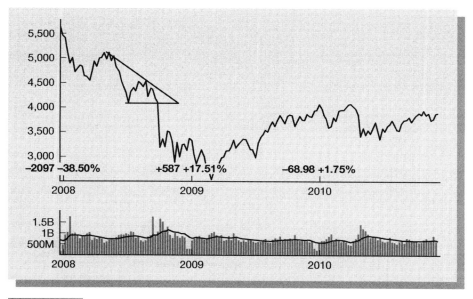

Figure 2.13   A descending triangle

Source: From CAC40, http://markets.ft.com/markets/interactiveChart.asp

Pennant

A pennant is like a triangle but involves a shorter-term congestion. A pennant is enclosed by two converging lines and is usually followed by the prevailing trend. (See Figure 2.14.)

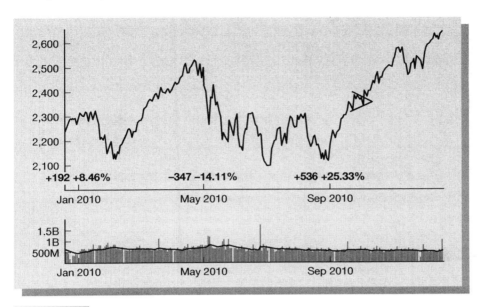

Figure 2.14   **A pennant**

Source: From Nasdaq, http://markets.ft.com/markets/interactiveChart.asp

Flag

A flag is a short-term congestion within narrow bands in the long-term trend. A flag is enclosed by parallel lines and is usually followed by the prevailing trend. (See Figure 2.15.)

Rectangle

A rectangle is a trading range enclosed by two parallel lines formed by at least two tops and two bottoms. (See Figure 2.16.)

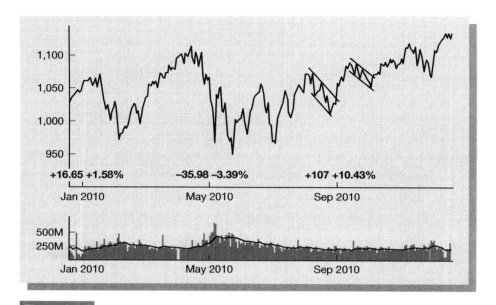

Figure 2.15   A flag

Source: From Eurofirst 300, http://markets.ft.com/markets/interactiveChart.asp

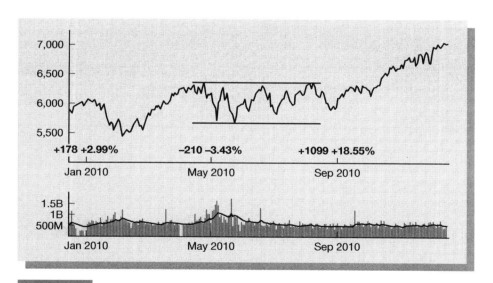

Figure 2.16   A rectangle

Source: From DAX, http://markets.ft.com/markets/interactiveChart.asp

Chapter review

▦ Reversal patterns are exhaustion price patterns from the prevailing trend and initiation of a new trend in the opposite direction. They include head and shoulders, tops and bottoms, rounded tops and rounded bottoms, and wedge reversals.

▦ Continuation patterns are congestion phases that occur within long-term trends. They include triangles, pennants, flags and rectangles.

▦ The objective of knowing these price patterns for range traders is for them to gauge the next support and resistance levels.

▦ The objective of knowing these price patterns for trend traders is for them to project potential profit so they can calculate the stop loss level at the point of entry.

A NOTE TO THE TRADING APPRENTICE

No one can predict the future with certainty – professional traders realise their mistakes early

Different traders will see different classical patterns in the same price series because pattern recognition is subjective and open to interpretation. Therefore, some people consider it to be an art. If it is a form of art, it is a very expensive and unproductive hobby because mistakenly recognising wrong patterns that are forming is very costly.

For example, what may be a rising wedge could also be a small symmetrical triangle or a pennant if the market continues to trend up. Therefore, although chartists agree on patterns that have already formed, they and the market rarely agree on the forming patterns. That is why no one can predict the future with certainty.

Professional traders will always recommend the more objective technical indicators. The technical indicators are mathematical formulas that have been well-researched and tested to have a positive statistical edge. Their chief concern is that what worked in the past may not continue to do so in the future. However, as the patterns show in this and the following chapters, history has a habit of repeating itself in prices.

3

Spot the bubbles and win

What topics are covered in this chapter?

In this chapter, we examine the different types of gap depending on their positions in the trend:

- exhaustion gap (island reversal)
- breakaway gap
- runaway gap
- common gap

What are the objectives?

The objectives of spotting a gap are:

- To determine if the old trend might be ending.
- To determine if a new trend might be beginning.

Introduction

Gaps at the bottom or top of charts are classical pattern formations that traders are always trying to spot. A gap is an empty space in the chart between the day's low (or high) and the previous day's high (or low). This gap signifies an overnight change when the local market is not trading. The following day, participants rush in to buy (or sell) at higher (or lower) prices than the previous day's close.

Exhaustion gap (island top reversal)

An island bottom reversal (exhaustion gap) is a bullish formation. An island bottom reversal is an area when the last sellers finish their selling. The exhaustion gap occurs after an extended period of a downtrend. The market gaps down lower on the opening, leaving the gap unfilled (the exhaustion gap) and no follow through selling occurs. The following day(s), the market gaps up, leaving the original gap unfilled. (See Figure 3.1.)

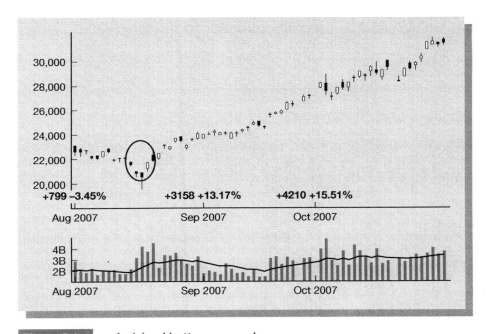

Figure 3.1   An island bottom reversal

Source: From Hang Seng, http://markets.ft.com/markets/interactiveChart.asp

An island top reversal (exhaustion gap) is a bearish formation and is an area when the last buyers finish their buying. The exhaustion gap occurs after an extended period of an uptrend. The market gaps up higher on the opening, leaving the gap unfilled (the exhaustion gap). No follow through buying occurs while earlier investors have exited or are exiting the market. The following day(s), the market gaps down, leaving the original gap unfilled. (See Figure 3.2.)

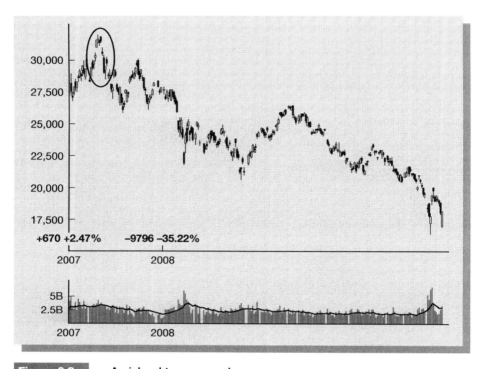

Figure 3.2   **An island top reversal**

Source: From Hang Seng, http://markets.ft.com/markets/interactiveChart.asp

Breakaway gap

A breakaway gap after a period of congestion signifies the beginning of a new trend if prices continue to move directionally. A breakaway gap occurs after a gap up above (or a gap down below) an extended trading range, leaving a gap with no trading activity. After a period of accumulation (or distribution), a new development happens when the local market is not trading and new buyers (or sellers) rush in to buy (or sell) the following day at prices higher (or lower) than the previous day's high (or low), resulting in a breakaway gap in the chart. If this gap is not filled, a breakaway gap occurs. Usually the breakaway gap signifies the beginning of a new trend, if the following day's prices continue to move in the same direction. (See Figure 3.3.)

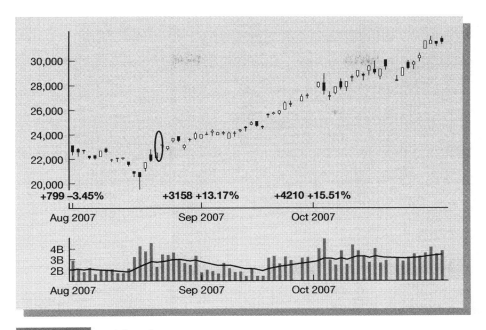

Figure 3.3   A breakaway gap

Source: From Hang Seng, http://markets.ft.com/markets/interactiveChart.asp

Runaway gap

A runaway gap is a continuation formation that occurs after the breakaway gap and signifies subsequent prices running away in the direction of the new trend. A runaway gap occurs after a gap up above (or a gap down below) the previous day's prices, leaving a gap with no trading activity. This happens when more new buyers (or sellers) rush in to buy (or sell) the following day at prices higher (or lower) than the previous day's high (or low), resulting in a runaway gap in the chart. This runaway gap confirms the beginning of a new trend, if the following day's prices continue to move in the same direction. (See Figure 3.4.)

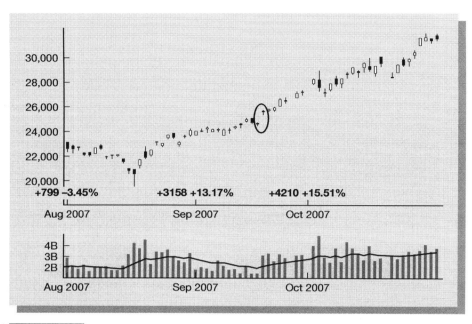

Figure 3.4   **A runaway gap**

Source: From Hang Seng, http://markets.ft.com/markets/interactiveChart.asp

Common gap

A common gap is a gap that occurs within a range but does not turn out to be a breakaway gap and therefore does not signify anything. (See Figure 3.5.)

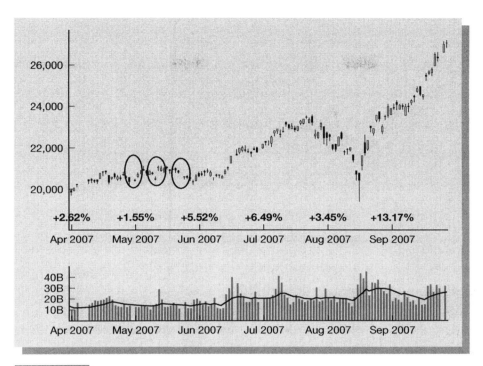

Figure 3.5   Common gaps

Source: From Hang Seng, http://markets.ft.com/markets/interactiveChart.asp

Chapter review

▦ An exhaustion gap is a reversal pattern that occurs after an extended trend and is usually followed by a reversal.

▦ A breakaway gap is a reversal pattern and occurs after a gap up above or a gap down below an extended trading range, leaving a gap with no trading activity.

▦ A runaway gap is a continuation pattern and occurs in mid-trend, after which the trend tends to accelerate faster in that direction.

▦ A common gap occurring within a trading range does not mean anything.

A NOTE TO THE TRADING APPRENTICE

Take note of trading gaps

If your technical indicator confirms it, a breakaway gap is the best pattern to trade. A breakaway (up) gap is also called 'rising window' in candlestick terminology. A breakaway (up) gap usually happens when the opening price and low price of the day are above the highs of the previous days when accumulation had occurred. If prices continue to rise above the resistance level, this represents the beginning of a new uptrend. This is the range breakout strategy that has been proved successful in many markets over the decades.

The breakaway (down) gap, also known as 'falling window', is the most exciting strategy in futures and short selling because when the market falls on panic selling, it crashes many percentage points in just a few days. This is when the asset, credit and confidence bubbles burst and is why I have called this chapter, 'Spot the bubbles and win'. If I were a graphic technician, this would be the foremost trading strategy I would use. However, as you will soon realise, I am a mechanical trader. It makes life very easy.

The drawback is that you do not know if the gap will be filled until the following day(s). If the price retraces back to fill the gap, the breakout is no longer valid. If the price does not retrace back to fill the gap, the chances are very good that a new long-term trend is beginning.

Therefore, you should initiate a position on identification of a new trend but always remember that half the time your entry will be wrong. This is a probability game and the probability is 50% that the market will move in the direction of your trade. If the market moves against you, cut your loss quickly. If the market moves in your favour, let the trend run its course. If there is a 50% chance of small losses and a 50% chance of huge gains, then the net trading experience will be large profits in the long run.

In the next chapter, we will go through what are considered some trend and profit-making opportunities. In the second part of this book, we approach professional model trading as a science subject where the pre-set trading rules are mathematical, systematic and objective. This is what I mean by being a mechanical trader and having an easy life.

4

Follow the winners: trading with the trend

What topics are covered in this chapter?

In this chapter, we examine range trading versus trend trading and consider:

- range
- support
- resistance
- range trading systems
- trend (uptrend and downtrend)
- channels (uptrend and downtrend)
- trend trading systems

What are the objectives?

- To know the definitions of support and resistance.
- To know how to use the definitions of support and resistance for range trading.
- To know how to use the definitions of support and resistance for trend trading.
- To know the definitions of uptrend and downtrend.
- To learn the trading systems to use for trend trading.

Introduction

The first decision a trader has to make is whether to trade within a range or to trade in and with a trend. A range is an area between support and resistance. The technique to trading in a range is to buy low at support and sell high at resistance.

The catch is that this method works about half the time: the other half, the market trends. This means that the range trader who bought low finds the prices trending down much lower or the range trader who sold high finds the prices trending up much higher.

Range

A range can be defined as an area that is enclosed by support at the bottom and resistance at the top. When prices are moving within a certain range, range trading techniques will apply. After a number of market observations have been recorded, technical analysis will look for bottoms as the support and tops as the resistance.

Classical technical analysis dictates that the price will tend to meet support at the lower end of the range and resistance at the upper end of the range. Classical technical analysis recommmends buying at the support/bottom of the range and selling at the resistance/top of the range.

Support

Support can be defined as the lower boundary of the trading range where the buying pressure is stronger than the selling pressure. The support level indicates the price level where the majority of traders believe that prices will move higher. Recognise that support can be encountered in the vicinity of previous major lows.

However, it is important to note that a prior low does not imply that a fall below that level is impossible. It simply indicates that some support is expected near the vicinity of the previous lows. It can fall through, by which time trend trading techniques should apply on the downward break.

In classical technical analysis, in range trading the technique is to buy at areas of support. The most basic trading tool to use is to draw a line at areas of previous lows, thus forming the area of support.

Exercise

1 Log on to http://markets.ft.com/markets/interactiveChart.asp

2 Select Nikkei; you should see a preconstructed line chart.

3 Move the cursor so that the horizontal support line touches two lows. (See Figure 4.1.)

4 (This is in line with the concept of double bottoms.)

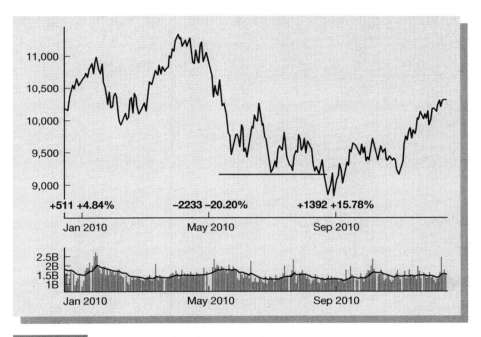

Figure 4.1   Chart showing the support line

Source: From Nikkei 225, http://markets.ft.com/markets/interactiveChart.asp

Following a period of sustained penetration below a prior low, the area of support can become an area of resistance when prices move up again later.

Now, with computer programs, one of the more sophisticated methods to identify support is to draw price envelope bands around the price structure. The lower boundary is defined as a certain distance below the mean or moving average. The distance away from the mean may be measured in terms of percentages or standard deviations.

Resistance

Resistance can be defined as the upper boundary of the trading range where the selling pressure is stronger than the buying pressure. The resistance level indicates the price at which the majority of traders believe that prices will move lower. Recognise that resistance can be encountered in the vicinity of previous major highs.

However, it is important to note that a prior high does not imply that a rally above that level is impossible. It simply indicates that some resistance is expected near the vicinity of the previous highs. It can rise through, by which time trend trading techniques should apply on the upward break.

1 Log on to http://markets.ft.com/markets/interactiveChart.asp

2 Select Nikkei; you should see a preconstructed line chart.

3 Move the cursor so that the horizontal resistance line touches two highs. (See Figure 4.2.)

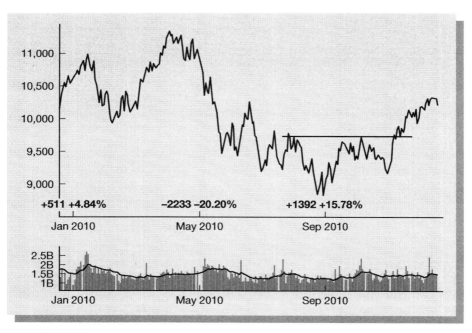

Figure 4.2   A chart showing the resistance line

Source: From Nikkei 225, http://markets.ft.com/markets/interactiveChart.asp

Following a period of sustained penetration above a prior high, the area of resistance becomes an area of support when prices move down again later.

In classical technical analysis, in range trading the trading technique is to sell at areas of resistance. The most basic trading tool to use is to draw a line at areas of previous highs, thus forming the area of resistance.

Again, one of the more sophisticated methods to identify resistance is to draw price envelope bands around the price structure. The upper boundary is defined as a certain distance above the mean or moving average. The distance away from the mean may be measured in terms of percentages or standard deviations.

Range trading systems

Generally, a range trading system is one that initiates a position in the opposite direction of a large price movement on the assumption that the market is due for correction.

Technically, there is no mechanical trading system for range trading. The support or the resistance that the trader chooses is arbitrary and differs from individual to individual.

Generally, range trading systems often appeal to new traders because their ultimate goal is to buy low and sell high. More experienced traders soon abandon range trading systems because these 'systems' do not include stops or limit losses and risks.

Trend

A trend can be defined as the general direction of the market. After a number of market observations have been recorded, technical analysis will look for breakouts from the trading range. It will also look for certain formations like downtrends and uptrends. (Downtrends and uptrends occur after breakouts from the trading range.)

Downtrend

A downtrend will form after the price falls below the most recent low or the horizontal support. A downtrend is characterised by lower highs and lower lows. In classical technical analysis, the most basic trading tool is to draw a straight downward sloping line tangential to several highs (at least two highs) in a down trend. A third point that is touching the straight line will confirm the validility of the downtrend. A downtrend line, therefore, is drawn connecting successively lower highs and remains intact until it is penetrated. A downtrend can be thought of as falling resistance levels: that is, the sellers/bears are in control and are pushing prices down.

Exercise

1. Log on to http://markets.ft.com/markets/interactiveChart.asp
2. Select Nikkei Index; you should see a preconstructed line chart.
3. Click on 'Trend Lines'.
4. Click the highest high, drag it to one of the lowest highs in the chart and click. Try to connect as many highs as possible. You will see that a downward sloping line is drawn. This is the downtrend line (see Figure 4.3).

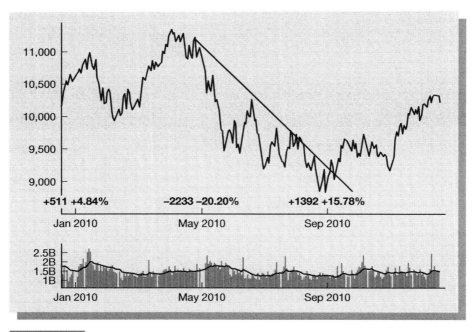

Figure 4.3   Chart showing downtrend line

Source: From Nikkei 225, http://markets.ft.com/markets/interactiveChart.asp

In trend trading, the trading technique in a downtrend is to enter sell short on confirmation of a downtrend (i.e lower highs and lower lows) and to exit on buy back when the price breaks up from the downtrend.

In contemporary technical analysis, the sophisticated method is to draw a moving average line or a price envelope similar to a standard deviation band below the moving average line (see Figure 4.4). A downtrend is confirmed when the prices are below the moving average and move towards the lower band. The distance away from the mean may be measured in terms of percentage or standard deviation.

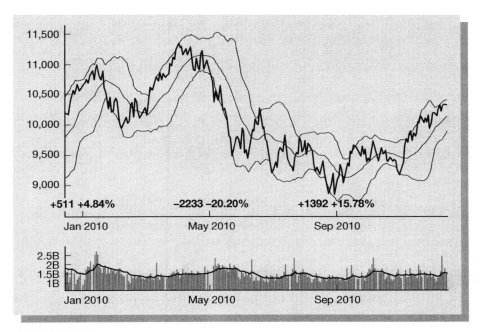

Figure 4.4   Chart showing downtrend using moving average and Bollinger bands

Source: From Nikkei 225 using Moving Average, http://markets.ft.com/markets/interactiveChart.asp

Uptrend

An uptrend will form after the price rises above the most recent high or the horizontal resistance. An uptrend is characterised by higher highs and higher lows. In classical technical analysis, the most basic trading tool is to draw a straight upward sloping line tangential to several lows (at least two lows) in an uptrend. A third point that is touching the straight line will confirm the validility of the uptrend. An uptrend line, therefore, is drawn connecting successively higher lows and remains intact until it is penetrated. A uptrend can be thought of as rising support levels: that is, the buyers/bulls are in control and are pushing prices higher.

Exercise

1 Log on to http://markets.ft.com/markets/interactiveChart.asp

2 Select Nikkei; you should see a preconstructed line chart.

3 Click on 'Trend Lines'.

4 Click the lowest low, drag it to one of the higher lows in the chart and click. Try to connect as many lows as possible. You will see that an upward sloping line is drawn. This is the uptrend line (see Figure 4.5).

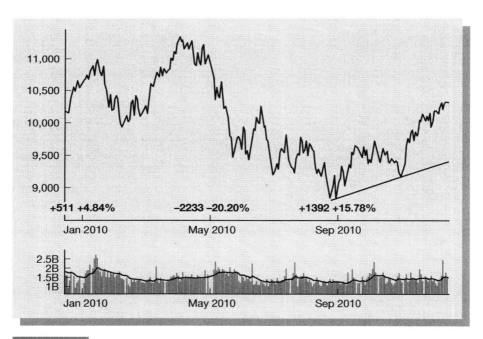

Figure 4.5   Chart showing uptrend line

Source: From Nikkei 225, http://markets.ft.com/markets/interactiveChart.asp

In trend trading, the trading technique in an uptrend is to enter buy long on confirmation of the uptrend (i.e higher highs and higher lows) and to exit on sell back when the price breaks down from the uptrend.

Once again the sophisticated method is to draw a moving average line or a price envelope similar to a standard deviation band above the moving average (see Figure 4.6). An uptrend is confirmed when prices move above the moving average and towards the upper band. The distance away from the mean may be measured in terms of percentage or standard deviation.

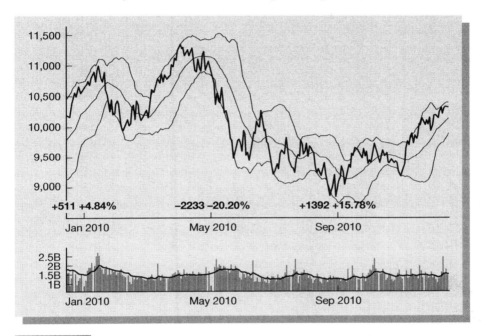

Figure 4.6   **Chart showing uptrend using moving average and Bollinger bands**

Source: From Nikkei 225, http://markets.ft.com/markets/interactiveChart.asp

Channels

Sometimes the lines connecting the highs and lows are roughly parallel, thus creating a channel formation. This indicates that the market is in a major downtrend or uptrend. Within these major channels, minor uptrend or downtrend lines can also be constructed.

Uptrend channel

An uptrend channel consists of two parallel lines that connect the highs on the top and the lows on the bottom, and is upward sloping (see Figure 4.7).

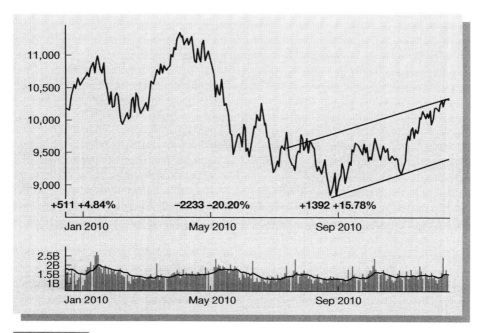

Figure 4.7   **Chart showing uptrend channel**

Source: From Nikkei 225, http://markets.ft.com/markets/interactiveChart.asp

Downtrend channel

A downtrend channel consists of two parallel lines that connect the highs on the top and the lows on the bottom and is downward sloping (see Figure 4.8).

Trend trading systems

Generally, a trend trading system initiates a position in the same direction as the current price movement on the assumption that the trend will continue. Technically, all mechanical trading systems are trend trading systems. They cater for trading only when there are trends in the market. Trend trading systems never sell at the high and never buy at the low, yet more experienced traders opt for trend trading systems because these systems are self-correcting in the sense that they include stops and limit risks. Thus losses are kept minimal while if there are trends, the profits are allowed to run.

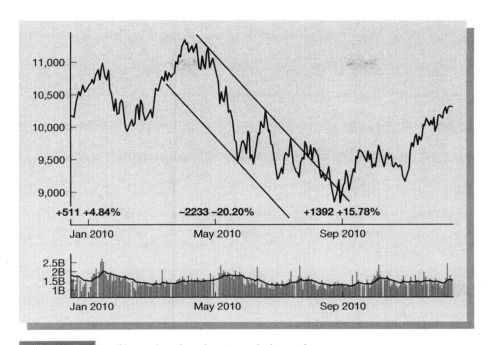

Figure 4.8   **Chart showing downtrend channel**

Source: From Nikkei 225, http://markets.ft.com/markets/interactiveChart.asp

Chapter review

- Price represents the fair market value as agreed between buyers and sellers.
- The support level is when there is a consensus between buyers and sellers that the price will not move lower as buyers outnumber sellers.
- The resistance level is when there is a consensus between buyers and sellers that the price will not move higher as sellers outnumber buyers.
- Successful penetration of the support level indicates that there is a change in traders' expectations. (i.e. traders expect prices to fall lower than the support level).
- Successful penetration of the resistance level indicates that there is a change in traders' expectations. (i.e. traders expect prices to rise higher than the resistance level).
- A trend represents a consistent change in prices. A downtrend is when there are lower highs and lower lows. There is a consensus between buyers and sellers that the price will not move higher than the pre-

vious high as sellers outnumber buyers. In a downtrend, the trading technique is to sell first and buy back when the price moves back above the downtrend line. In classical technical analysis, the trading tool to use involves drawing a straight downward sloping line touching two or more highs as the downtrend line. In contemporary technical analysis, the trading tool to use involves drawing a moving average line or a price band below the moving average line. When the price moves down below the moving average line and towards/below the lower band, the trading technique is to sell. (A downtrend can also be thought of as declining resistance levels – the sellers/bears are in control and are pushing the prices lower.)

▓ An uptrend is when there are higher highs and higher lows. There is a consensus between buyers and sellers that the price will not move lower than the previous low as buyers outnumber sellers. In an uptrend, the trading technique is to buy first and sell back when the price moves back below the uptrend line. In classical technical analysis, the trading tool to use involves drawing a straight upward sloping line touching two or more lows as the uptrend line. In contemporary technical analysis, the trading tool to use involves drawing a moving average line or a price band above the moving average line. When the price moves up above the moving average line and towards/above the upper band, the trading technique is to buy. (An uptrend can also be thought of as rising support levels – the buyers/bulls are in control and are pushing the prices higher.)

▓ Successful penetration of the uptrend indicates that there is a change in traders' expectations. (i.e. traders expect prices to fall lower than the support level).

▓ Successful penetration of the downtrend indicates that there is a change in traders' expectations. (i.e. traders expect prices to rise higher than the resistance level).

▓ Mechanical trading systems can be easily devised for trend trading. Such systems will give enter signals (buy or sell) and exit signals (sell or buy). A mechanical buy will emerge when the price breaks up from the downtrend line and upon confirmation of an uptrend. An exit sell signal will emerge when the price breaks down from the uptrend line. A mechanical sell will emerge when the price breaks down from the uptrend line and upon confirmation of a downtrend. An exit buy signal will emerge when the price breaks up from the downtrend line.

A NOTE TO THE TRADING APPRENTICE

Support and resistance levels are very important decision-making points – they can make or break your trading career

Most professional traders trade on trends. Trading methods can be categorised into:

▓ **Range trading** – to trade within a certain range between the area of support and the area of resistance. The range trading technique is to recognise areas of support to buy and areas of resistance to sell. Classical technical analysis focuses a lot on support and resistance.

▓ **Trend trading** – to trade below the area of support and above the area of resistance. The trend trading technique is to recognise where the area of breakout (down) below the support is to sell and the area of breakout (up) above the resistance is to buy.

Classical range trading recommends that you buy low at the support and sell high at the resistance, which is completely opposed to contemporary trend trading which is to buy high at the breakout from the resistance and sell back higher, and to sell low at the breakout from the support and buy back lower.

The difference between a successful trader and an unsuccessful trader is the ability to recognise range trading from trend trading and apply the right trading tools at the appropriate time.

Generally, range trading sytems often appeal to new traders because their ultimate goal is to buy low and sell high. More experienced traders soon abandon range trading systems because these 'systems' do not include stops or limit losses and risks.

Support and resistance levels are often broken when there are big strong directional price movements. Prices can break decisively out of the trading range when there are big trend movements. When prices break out of the trading range, range trading techniques are no longer valid.

Contemporary technical analysis recommends that you buy when the price breaks above the upper end of the range (in an uptrend) and sell when the price breaks below the lower end of the range (in a downtrend). Contemporary technical analysis concentrates more on trend trading. Contemporary quantitative technical analysis uses technical indicators, which we will meet in the next chapter, to identify and trade on trends.

5

The tools that professionals use

What topics are covered in this chapter?

There are two groups of technical indicators:

▓ lagging technical indicators

▓ leading technical indicators

Here we examine the lagging technical indicators:

▓ simple moving average

▓ exponential moving average

▓ moving average convergence divergence (MACD)

Leading indicators are examined in the next chapter.

What are the objectives?

The objectives of calculating and using moving averages are:

▓ To smoothen out fluctuations and see the underlying directional trend.

Introduction

A technical indicator is a technical analysis tool used by traders and is often used in trading systems to give appropriate buy or sell signals. A technical indicator is defined as a mathematical calculation that can be applied to market prices. The result is a value that can be used to anticipate changes in prices.

Simple moving average

The moving average is one of the most important tools of technical analysis. Moving average can be defined as the average price at any given time, and refers to a set of numbers being averaged continuously while moving through time. The moving average, therefore, reflects the trend in the price series by smoothing out meaningless fluctuations in the data.

In a range trading market, the moving average tends to oscillate in a sideways pattern while in a trend trading market, the moving average tends to move in a definite upward or downward direction. Therefore, in a trend trading market, the moving average may be used as a technical indicator to give a buy or sell signal.

Finally, the moving average represents the consensus of investors' expectations over a given period.

The formula

A simple moving average is calculated by adding up the prices for the most recent n days and then dividing the sum total by n. The number of days (n) determines how sensitive the moving average is.

Example

A three-day simple moving average on 17/12/2010 is calculated by adding up:

15/12/2010	1,235.23
16/12/2010	1,242.87
17/12/2010	1,243.91
	3,722.01

and then dividing 3,722.01 by 3 = 1,240.67.

Exercise

1 Log on to http://markets.ft.com/markets/interactiveChart.asp

2 Select S&P 500; you should see a preconstructed line chart.

3 Select 'Add Indicators' at the top, left-hand corner.

4 Select 'Upper Indicators' and then 'Simple Moving Average'.

5 This will give you a 50-day moving average.

6 If you want to change that to a standard 20-day moving average, click 'Edit' and change the number of days to 20.

The result is shown in Figure 5.1.

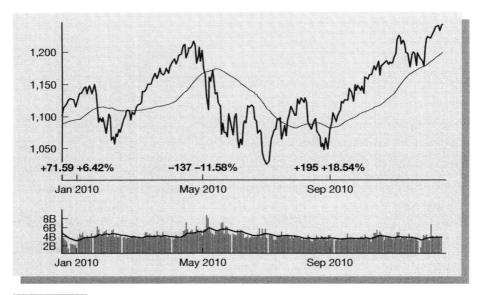

Figure 5.1   **Chart showing a simple moving average**
Source: From S&P 500, http://markets.ft.com/markets/interactiveChart.asp

In this example, the 50-day simple moving average is a fitting example to use because it touches several tops and bottoms without crossing them unnecessarily, thus preventing some whipsaws (entries that result in losses).

Sell signal

If the market price is lower than the simple moving average, the market's current expectation can be viewed as being lower than its average expectation over the last *n* days – the market is increasingly bearish. In a trending market, the trading technique when the market price is lower than the simple moving average is to sell.

Buy signal

If the market price is higher than the simple moving average, the market's current expectation can be viewed as being higher than its average expectation over the last *n* days – the market is increasingly bullish. In a trending market, the trading technique when the market price is higher than the simple moving average is to buy.

Exponential moving average (EMA)

An exponential moving average gives more weight to most current prices and diminishes the importance of older prices exponentially. It therefore tracks current price movements more closely than a simple moving average.

Exercise

1 Log on to http://markets.ft.com/markets/interactiveChart.asp

2 Select S&P 500; you should see a preconstructed line chart.

3 Select 'Add Indicators' at the top, left-hand corner.

4 Select 'Upper Indicators' and then 'Exponential Moving Average'.

5 This will give you a 50-day exponential moving average.

6 If you want to change that to a 20-day exponential moving average, click 'Edit' and change the number of days to 20.

The result is shown in Figure 5.2.

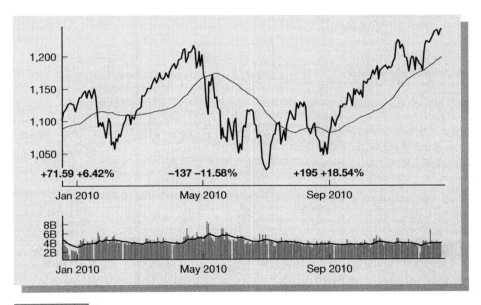

Figure 5.2   Chart showing an exponential moving average

Source: From S&P 500, http://markets.ft.com/markets/interactiveChart.asp

Sell signal

If the market price is lower than the exponential moving average, the market's current expectation can be viewed as being increasingly bearish. In a trending market, the trading technique when the market price is lower than the exponential moving average is to sell.

Buy signal

If the market price is higher than the exponential moving average, the market's current expectation can be viewed as being increasingly bullish. In a trending market, the trading technique when the market price is higher than the exponential moving average is to buy.

Moving average convergence divergence (MACD)

Exponential moving averages are used to construct a momentum oscillator called moving average convergence divergence (MACD). MACD was created by Gerald Appel, author of *Technical Analysis, Power Tools for Active Investors* (2005).

Formula

The MACD line can be constructed in the following way:

■ Compute the exponential moving average for 12 periods (EMA12).

■ Compute the exponential moving average for 26 periods (EMA26).

■ Take the difference between the exponential moving averages of 12 periods and 26 periods (EMA12-EMA26).

The signal line can be constructed in the following way:

■ Compute the simple nine periods moving average for the difference between EMA12 and EMA26.

Exercise

1 Log on to http://markets.ft.com/markets/interactiveChart.asp

2 Select S&P 500; you should see a preconstructed line chart.

3 Select 'Add Indicators' at the top, left-hand corner.

4 Select 'Lower Indicators' and then 'MACD'.

5 This will give you the MACD lines at the bottom of the chart.

The result is shown in Figure 5.3.

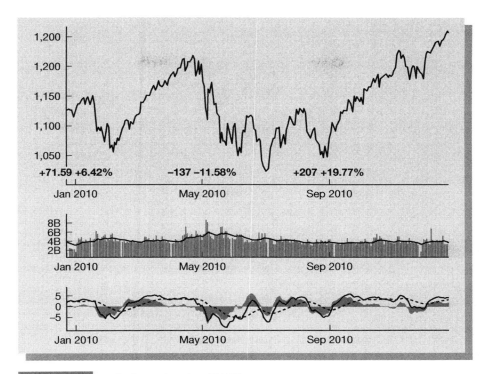

Figure 5.3   A chart showing MACD

Source: From S&P 500, http://markets.ft.com/markets/interactiveChart.asp

Buy signal

When the MACD is above the signal line, the trading technique is to buy.

Sell signal

When the MACD line is below the signal line, the trading technique is to sell.

The MACD histogram is constructed from the difference between the MACD indicator and the signal line. The shape of the histogram indicates the possible direction that the trend might be heading.

Chapter review

▓ A technical indicator is a mathematical formula used in trading systems to generate appropriate buy or sell signals.

▓ A moving average is a specific set of numbers that are averaged continuously while moving through time. As such, a moving average is a lagging indicator. The moving average, therefore, reflects the trend in the price series by smoothing out meaningless fluctuations in the data. There are many variations of moving average including simple moving average and exponential moving average.

▓ If the current market price is above the moving average, the market sentiment is increasingly bullish. If the current market price is below the moving average, the market sentiment is increasingly bearish.

▓ Moving average crossover occurs when a shorter-term moving average crosses a longer-term moving average. A buy signal emerges when the shorter-term moving average is above the longer-term moving average. A sell signal emerges when the shorter-term moving average is below the longer-term moving average.

▓ The main weaknesses of moving average indicators are that they lag behind major turning points by a few periods and that they are trend following indicators, which will generate a lot of false entries in range trading markets.

▓ The moving average convergence divergence (MACD), another lagging indicator, is constructed by:

– computing the exponential moving average for 12 periods (EMA12)

– computing the exponential moving average for 26 periods (EMA26)

– taking the difference between the exponential moving averages of 12 periods and 26 periods (EMA12-EMA26).

▓ To obtain buy or sell signals, another reference line called the signal line is constructed by computing the simple nine-periods moving average for the difference between EMA12 and EMA26. If the MACD is above the signal line, a buy signal emerges; if it is below the signal line, a sell signal emerges.

A NOTE TO THE TRADING APPRENTICE

The weaknesses of moving averages as technical indicators for trading systems

The main weaknesses of the moving average are that:

▦ it is a lagging indicator so turning points will always lag behind the corresponding transition in the current price series, and

▦ while it tends to do well in a trending market, it generates a lot of false signals in a range market.

Some trend traders prefer to take a holiday during a range market to avoid these whipsaws. A range market usually happens when the moving average is flattish. You may use several moving averages to determine if the market is in a range or you may use envelope bands around the moving average to define range trading areas. We will be discussing envelope bands in range breakout later.

6

Leading technical indicators in the market

What topics are covered in this chapter?

The leading technical indicators covered here are:

- momentum
- relative strength index (RSI)
- directional movement (DM)
- parabolic stop and reverse (SAR)
- stochastics
- on balance volume (OBV).

What are the objectives?

- To anticipate overbought market conditions and generate a sell signal accordingly.
- To anticipate oversold market conditions and generate a buy signal accordingly.

Introduction

It is important to know about the leading indicators that other world traders use so that we can anticipate the next wave of buying on support or selling on resistance. A leading indicator anticipates if the market is overbought or oversold.

A leading indicator based on momentum is called an oscillator. Momentum is the rate of change.

Momentum

The simplest momentum calculation is the difference between today's close and the close n days ago.

Example

The three-day momentum is the difference between today's close at 1,016.5 and the close three days ago at 1,002.0, which is 14.5.

Graphically, this can be depicted by a horizontal median also called the equilibrium line. When the momentum is above the equilibrium line, the current price is higher than the price three days ago. When the momentum is above the equilibrium line and rising, prices are advancing with increasing momentum. An extreme momentum reading above the equilibrium line indicates an overbought level.

When the momentum is below the equilibrium line, the current price is lower than the price three days ago. When the momentum is below the equilibrium line and falling, prices are dropping with increasing momentum. An extreme momentum reading below the equilibrium line indicates an oversold level.

As with moving averages, the number of days, n, used in an oscillator determines how sensitive the indicator will be.

Exercise

1 Log on to http://markets.ft.com/markets/interactiveChart.asp
2 Select S&P 500; you should see a preconstructed line chart.
3 Select 'Add Indicators' at the top, left-hand corner.
4 Select 'Lower Indicators' and then 'Momentum'.
5 This will give you Momentum at the bottom of the chart (See Figure 6.1).

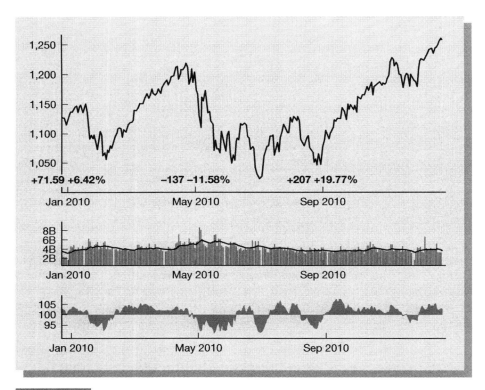

Figure 6.1   **A chart showing the momentum indicator**

Source: From S&P 500, http://markets.ft.com/markets/interactiveChart.asp

Relative strength index (RSI)

RSI is a leading indicator that was introduced by J. Welles Wilder Jr. in his book *New Concepts in Technical Trading Systems*. He introduced the world to many truly innovative and original concepts such as relative strength index (RSI), directional movement (DM) and parabolic stop and reverse (SAR). Relative strength is the average of days that the market closes up divided by the average of days that the market closes down.

Up days = Current day's close > Previous day's close

Down days = Current day's close < Previous day's close

Example

The relative strength (RS) for 14 days (in which six are up days and eight are down days) is

$$RS_{14} = \frac{\sum (6 \text{ days' closes}) / 14}{\sum (8 \text{ days' closes}) / 14}$$

RSI is simply an index of RS and shows overbought or oversold market conditions:

$$RSI = 100 - [100/(1 + RS)]$$

Exercise

1 Log on to http://markets.ft.com/markets/interactiveChart.asp
2 Select S&P 500; you should see a preconstructed line chart.
3 Select 'Add Indicators' at the top, left-hand corner.
4 Select 'Lower Indicators' and then 'Relative Strength Index'.
5 This will give you RSI, overbought and oversold levels at the bottom of the chart (see Figure 6.2).

Buy signal

Any RSI value below 30 is considered oversold and a possible bottom is indicated. The trading technique is to look for a point, along with other confirmation signals, at which to buy. Note that RSI can remain below 30 for days and those who buy early using this signal alone might end up catching a falling market.

Sell signal

Any RSI value above 70 is considered overbought and a possible top is indicated. The trading technique is to look for a point, along with other confirmation signals, at which to sell. Note that RSI can remain above 70 for days and those who sell early using this signal alone might end up seeing the market continue to rise.

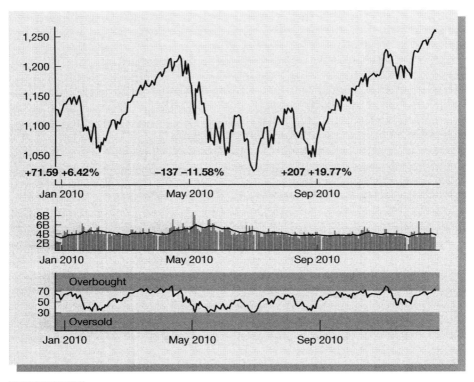

Figure 6.2   A chart showing RSI

Source: From S&P 500, http://markets.ft.com/markets/interactiveChart.asp

Directional movement (DM)

Directional movement, as developed by Welles Wilder, consists of:

▧ the average directional index (ADX)

▧ the positive directional index (+DI)

▧ the negative directional index (–DI).

ADX is the 14-day average of the directional movement index (DX) that is made up of the positive directional index (+DI) – an indication of the percentage of the total true range of the last 14 days which was up – and the negative directional index (–DI) – an indication of the percentage of the total true range of the last 14 days which was down.

$$DX = \frac{[(+DI) - (-DI)]}{[(+DI) + (-DI)]} \times 100$$

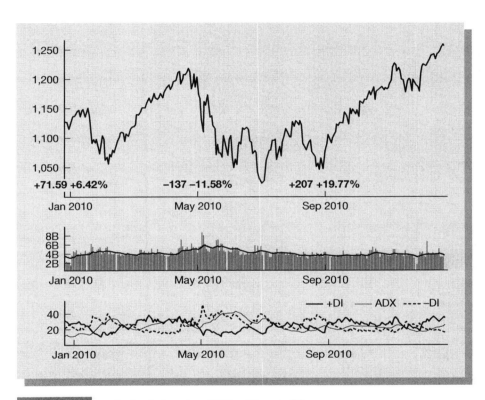

Figure 6.3   A chart showing ADX, +DI and –DI

Source: From S&P 500, http://markets.ft.com/markets/interactiveChart.asp

Buy signal

When +DI is more than –DI, a buy signal is considered probable in an uptrend.

Sell signal

When –DI is more than +DI, a sell signal is considered probable in a downtrend.

Parabolic stop and reverse (SAR)

Parabolic SAR is another leading indicator that was developed by Welles Wilder. Parabolic SAR is a function of price and time and can be used to set trailing stops for long and short positions.

Exercise

1   Log on to http://markets.ft.com/markets/interactiveChart.asp
2   Select S&P 500; you should see a preconstructed line chart.
3   Select 'Add Indicators' at the top, left-hand corner.
4   Select 'Upper Indicators' and then 'Parabolic SAR'.
5   Parabolic SAR indicator values are plotted as dots above and below the close price line (see Figure 6.4).

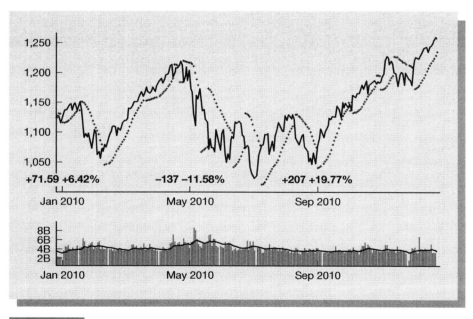

Figure 6.4   **A chart showing parabolic SAR**

Source: From S&P 500, http://markets.ft.com/markets/interactiveChart.asp

Long positions

For long positions, the dotted lines below the prices signify possible points to put trailing stops.

Short positions

For short positions, the dotted lines above the prices signify possible points to put trailing stops.

At the beginning of the trend, parabolic SAR shows a greater distance between the price and the trailing stop. As the trend progresses, the distance narrows and the trailing stop is tightened (especially when the trend is changing).

Stochastics

Stochastics is a leading indicator developed by George Lane to measure momentum.[1] It compares the difference between the current close to the low in a given period to the absolute price range in this given period. This is called %K.

$$\%K = 100 * (C - L)/(H - L)$$

where:

C = current close

H = high in n periods

L = low in n periods

%D also takes the average of %K (the default is three days).

$$\%D = \frac{\sum(3 \text{ period } \%K)}{3}$$

---

[1] His article 'Lane's Stochastics' is published in the second issue of *Technical Analysis of Stocks and Commodities* (1984).

1 Log on to http://markets.ft.com/markets/interactiveChart.asp

2 Select S&P 500; you should see a preconstructed line chart.

3 Select 'Add Indicators' at the top, left-hand corner.

4 Select 'Lower Indicators' and then 'Fast Stochastic'. See Figure 6.5.

5 Select 'Lower Indicators' and then 'Slow Stochastic'.

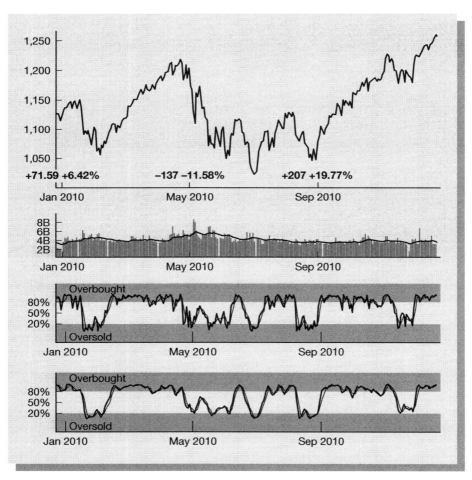

Figure 6.5   **A chart showing stochastics**

Source: From S&P 500, http://markets.ft.com/markets/interactiveChart.asp

Buy signal

Any stochastic value below 20 is considered oversold and the trading technique is to look for a point along with other confirmation signals to buy. When the price makes a new low and %D makes a higher low than previously, a bullish divergence is indicated. The buy signal emerges when the K line crosses the D line at the bottom.

Sell signal

Any stochastic value above 80 is considered overbought and the trading technique is to look for a point along with other confirmation signals to sell. When the price makes a new high and %D makes a lower high than previously, a bearish divergence is indicated. The sell signal emerges when the K line crosses the D line at the top.

On balance volume (OBV)

OBV[2] is a leading indicator developed by Joseph Granville to determine the level of accumulation or distribution by comparing volume to price movement. OBV charts an increasing cumulative volume as the price closes up, and a decreasing cumulative volume as the price closes down.

▩ If the current close is higher than the previous close:

OBV = OBV (previous period) + Volume (current period)

▩ If the current close is lower than the previous close:

OBV = OBV (previous period) – Volume (current period)

▩ If the current close is equal to the previous close:

OBV = OBV (previous period)

The line that OBV forms can be used to look for confirmation or divergence.

---

[2] OBV was originally called 'Cumulative volume' by Woods and Vignolia before Granville called it 'on balance volume' in his book *Granville's New Key to Stock Market Profits* (1963).

1 Log on to http://markets.ft.com/markets/interactiveChart.asp
2 Select S&P 500; you should see a preconstructed line chart.
3 Select 'Add Indicators' at the top, left-hand corner.
4 Select 'Lower Indicators' and then 'On Balance Volume'.
5 This will give you an OBV line at the bottom of the chart (see Figure 6.6).

Uptrend

If OBV is rising at an increasing rate (volume is increasing) and prices are
rising, OBV serves as a confirmation signal of an uptrend.

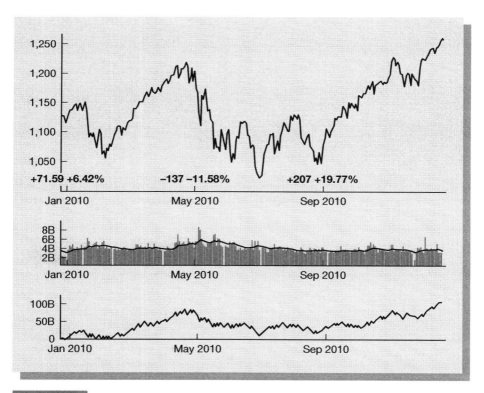

Figure 6.6   A chart showing on balance volume (OBV)
Source: From S&P 500, http://markets.ft.com/markets/interactiveChart.asp

If OBV is rising at a decreasing rate (volume is declining) and prices are rising, OBV serves as a divergence sign that the uptrend is not sustainable.

Downtrend

If OBV is falling at an increasing rate (volume is increasing) and prices are falling, OBV serves as a confirmation signal of a downtrend.

If OBV is falling at a decreasing rate (volume is declining) and prices are falling, OBV serves as a divergence sign that the downtrend is not sustainable.

Chapter review

▦ An oscillator is based on momentum (rate of change) and therefore is a leading indicator. The simplest momentum calculation is the difference between today's closing price and the closing price n days ago. Graphically, this can be depicted by a horizontal median also called the equilibrium line. When the momentum is above the equilibrium line and rising, prices are advancing with an increasing momentum. An extreme momentum reading above the equilibrium line indicates an overbought level. When the momentum is below the equilibrium line and falling, prices are falling with increasing momentum. An extreme momentum reading below the equilibrium line indicates an oversold level.

▦ Relative strength index (RSI) is a leading indicator. Any RSI value below 30 is considered oversold and the trading technique is to look for a point and other confirmation signals to buy. Any RSI value above 70 is considered overbought and the trading technique is to look for a point and other confirmation signals to sell.

▦ Average directional index (ADX) is developed to evaluate the strength of the current trend. ADX is derived from +DI and –DI. A buy signal occurs when +DI > –DI. A sell signal occurs when –DI > +DI. If ADX > 40, the trend is strong. If ADX < 20, the trend is weak.

▦ Parabolic SAR is used to set trailing stops. In an uptrend, the dotted lines below the price are used for trailing stops. In a downtrend, the dotted lines above the price are used for trailing stops.

▦ Stochastics is another leading indicator. Any value below 20 is considered oversold and the trading technique is to look for other confirmation signals to buy. Any value above 80 is considered overbought and the trading technique is to look for other confirmation signals to sell.

▨ On balance volume (OBV) is used to chart increasing cumulative volume when the price closes up. OBV charts decreasing cumulative volume when the price closes down. If volume is increasing, OBV is rising at an accelerating rate and prices are rising, this is confirmation of an uptrend. However, if volume is declining, OBV is rising at a decreasing rate, even though prices are rising, this is a divergence sign that the uptrend is not sustainable. If volume is increasing, OBV is falling at an accelerating rate and prices are falling, this is confirmation of a downtrend. However, if volume is declining, OBV is falling at a decreasing rate, even though prices are falling, this is a divergence sign that the downtrend is not sustainable.

A NOTE TO THE TRADING APPRENTICE

Weaknesses of oscillators as technical indicators for a trading system

Academic studies on historical prices generally show that oscillators such as momentum, RSI and parabolic fail to generate better than buy-and-hold policy returns. These oscillators are predictive. They signal the first signs of divergence that may or may not come to pass, therefore they are not as reliable as historical prices or lagging indicators, like moving averages, which try to confirm the trend.

Beware and be aware when using oscillators. I do not use leading indicators and do not advise the trading apprentice to start with this habit. However, the concept of mathematical formulas for technical indicators is very good and is a good habit to adopt as we design, construct and test technical indicators for mechanical trading systems.

Let us start, in the next chapter, with simple, easy-to-use and profitable systems including range breakout.

7

The profit opportunities

What topics are covered in this chapter?

There are various methods that employ this range breakout strategy. The strategy is essentially the same regardless of what it is called – you buy or sell on breakout:

- absolute range breakout
- fixed percentage (price envelope) band breakout
- bollinger bands
- volatility breakout.

What are the objectives?

The objectives of defining breakout systems are:

- to determine the breakout point according to a mathematical algorithm
- to use a constant x% or standard deviation bands.

Introduction

The market is either trading in a range or it has broken out of the range into a trend. The defining moment occurs when it is breaking out of the current range into a new trend. A trading-range breakout system, a trading system that emits a signal upon breaking out of the range, is the simplest mechanical trading system. Point and figure, as well as Kagi, employ this method for generating buy and sell signals.

When the current price breaks out of the trading range as signified by the last high (or *x* number of periods high), the trading signal is to buy. When the current price breaks out of the trading range as signified by the last low (or *x* number of periods low), the trading signal is to sell.

Absolute range breakout

A 20-day breakout system is to buy on breakup above the last 20 days trading range and to sell on breakdown below the last 20 days trading range. If the market price is higher than any other prices in the last 20 days, the signal is to buy. If the market price is lower than any other prices in the last 20 days, the signal is to sell.

If the market price is still within the 20-day range, volatility is low. There is no volatility breakout. Therefore, in a trend trading system, there is no signal to buy or to sell.

If the market price is outside the 20-day range, volatility is high. There is a signal to buy if the market price is higher than the highest price in the last 20 days. There is a signal to sell if the market price is lower than the lowest price in the last 20 days.

Example

If the market price is lower than any other prices in the last 20 days, the signal is to sell. In Figure 7.1, on 27/4/2010, the low, 5,533.5 is lower than any other prices or lows in the last 20 days, so we sell. When the market price on 27/4/2010 passes the lowest price on 31/3/2010, which was at 5,646.0, the trading decision is to sell.

If the market price is higher than any other prices in the last 20 days, the signal is to buy. In Figure 7.1, on 17/6/2010, the high, 5,294.0 is higher than any other prices or highs in the last 20 days, so the signal is to buy. When the market price on 17/6/2010 passes the highest high on 3/6/2010, which was at 5,262.50, the trading decision is to buy back.

If on 27/4/2010 you sold at 5,646.0 and on 17/6/2010 you bought back at 5,262.5, your trading gain is 383.5.

Note that in futures contracts you can sell short first and buy back later.

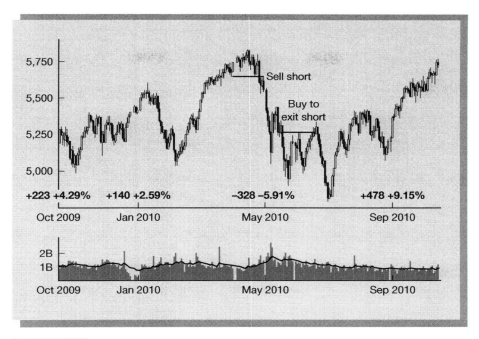

Figure 7.1   Candlestick chart showing 20-day breakout

Source: From FTSE 100, http://markets.ft.com/markets/interactiveChart.asp

Other forms of trading-range breakout are breakouts from bands. The bands may be a constant *x*% from the moving average band or they may be standard deviation (volatility) bands.

Fixed percentage (price envelope) band breakout

Fixed percentage trading bands are sometimes referred to as the moving average envelope. Fixed percentage trading bands are created from the moving average. The middle band is therefore the moving average; the upper band is the moving average extended upwards by *x*%; the lower band is the moving average extended downwards by *x*%. The fixed percentage trading bands are initially used by Dow theorists to avoid trading (whipsaws) when the moving average is flat (when the market is ranging).

Dow theorists use the upper band as a confirmation of the buy signal and the lower band as a confirmation of the sell signal. They do not trade when the market is ranging between the upper band and the lower band. The percentage set is completely arbitrary and should be set theoretically to encompass all the prices when the market is ranging.

After the moving average line is drawn, the $x\%$ of moving average may be calculated and:

▪ added onto the moving average to form the upper $x\%$ moving average band and

▪ subtracted from the moving average to form the lower $x\%$ moving average band.

If the percentage is set wide enough, the bands should cover most observations. Some novice traders would be tempted to use the upper band as resistance and a possible point to sell, and the lower band as support and a possible point to buy. However, on closer observation it can be seen that this strategy does not always make a profit and the potential losses are huge as there is no inherent, in-built risk control mechanism.

Exercise

1 In http://markets.ft.com/markets/interactiveChart.asp, click on 'Add Indicators'.

2 Select 'Upper Indicators'.

3 Choose 'Moving Average Envelope' and you should get Moving Average Envelope (20, 6).

A moving average envelope (20, 6) refers to 6% bands above and below the 20-day moving average (see Figure 7.2). It can also be seen that the $x\%$ bands do not fit the price series well. A better fit may be to use volatility to define the trading range.

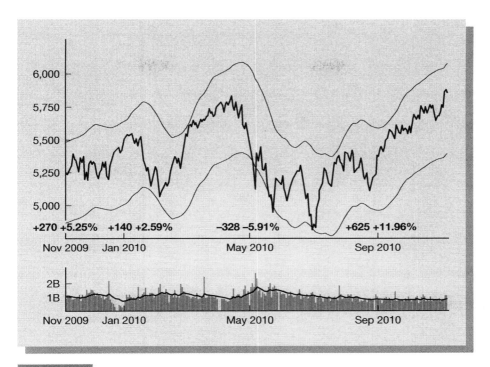

Figure 7.2   A chart showing the moving average envelope

Source: From FTSE 100, http://markets.ft.com/markets/interactiveChart.asp

Volatility

Volatility may be defined as how prices move in relation to the mean, whether they move far apart from the mean or their movements are very erratic. Statistically, volatility is measured by variance and standard deviation. These can be used as technical indicators to make trading decisions.

Variance calculates the possible variations from the mean (average). The mathematical formula for variance is:

$$\sigma^2 = \sum \frac{(x - \bar{x})^2}{n}$$

Standard deviation is another statistical measure of volatility. Standard deviation can be defined as the possible deviations from the moving average. Statistically, standard deviation calculates the range of possible values from the mean (average).

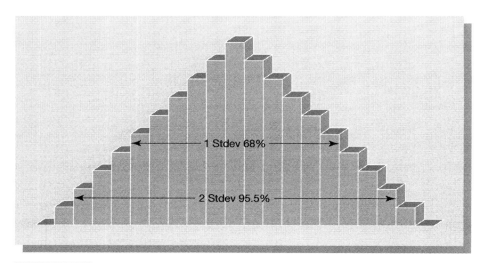

Figure 7.3   **The normal distribution showing one and two standard deviations**

The mathematical formula for standard deviation is:

$$\sigma = \sqrt{\sum \frac{(x - \bar{x})^2}{n}}$$

In statistics, if the data are normal, a normal bell shape curve would form for the distribution of the frequency of the data (see Figure 7.3). According to statistical theory, about 68% of all observations fall within one standard deviation of the mean and about 95% of all observations fall within two standard deviations.

There is more on volatility later in the chapter.

Bollinger bands

In technical analysis, a two standard deviation band system was created by John Bollinger for use as a technical tool. These bands can be viewed as an adaptation of the early trading bands of constant x% from the moving average bands used at that time to cover most observations. Two standard deviation bands from a 20-day moving average fitted the criterion because the area between the upper band and the lower band covers 95.5% of observations. These two bands were named Bollinger bands.[3]

---

[3] In his book *Bollinger on Bollinger Bands*, John Bollinger recounts how these bands are derived and how they got their name.

Bollinger bands consist of a set of three lines drawn around the price structure. The middle band is a simple moving average, which serves as the central reference for the upper and lower bands. The areas between the upper and lower bands and the middle band are determined by the standard deviation of the same data that were used for the average. The default parameters are 20 periods and two standard deviations and they may be adjusted to suit your trading purpose.

■ The middle Bollinger band = 20-period simple moving average
■ The upper Bollinger band = 20-period simple moving average + (2 × 20-period standard deviation)
■ The lower Bollinger band = 20-period simple moving average – (2 × 20-period standard deviation)

The purpose of Bollinger bands is to provide definitions of relative high and relative low. Prices are considered relatively high at the upper band and relatively low at the lower band.

Exercise

1 In http://markets.ft.com/markets/interactiveChart.asp, click on 'Add Indicators'.
2 Select 'Upper Indicators'.
3 Choose 'Bollinger bands' and you should get Bollinger bands (20, 2).

Bollinger bands (20, 2) refers to the two standard deviation bands above and below the 20-day moving average. (See Figure 7.4.)

Uses of volatility as a technical indicator

Volatility is low when the market is in range trading. The trading technique would be to sell at the relative high, which according to some traders is at the upper two standard deviations band. The trading technique would be to buy at the relative low, which according to some traders is at the lower two standard deviations band. However, according to finance theory, low risk (as measured by low volatility) results in low return (as measured by low profit).

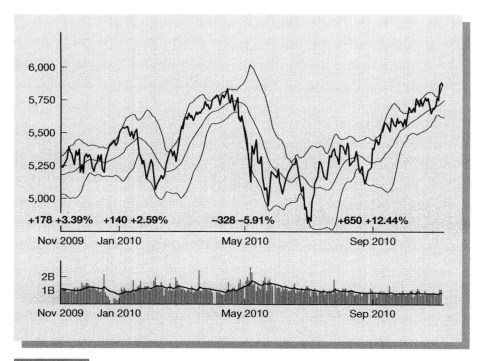

Figure 7.4   **A chart showing Bollinger bands**

Source: From FTSE 100, http://markets.ft.com/markets/interactiveChart.asp

As professional traders, we are not interested in low returns. We are only interested in high returns, which are usually accompanied by high risk (as measured by high volatility). Volatility is high when the market is out of range trading; when it is trend trading. The trading technique is to buy on breakup of a range as defined by the one standard deviation upper band and to sell on breakdown of a range as defined by the one standard deviation lower band.

This mechanical trading system can be called a volatility breakout system. Note that these systems work for those instruments that can be short sold.

Volatility breakout

Generally, a common volatility breakout system defines the upper and lower boundaries of a trading range (this can be a day or a week's trading range) for it to break out of. If it breaks up above a certain percentage of that range, the signal is to buy. If it breaks down below a certain percentage of that range, the signal is to sell. This is the basis of some mathematical trading models.

Another type of volatility breakout system is BBZ. If the price breaks above the +1 standard deviation level, the signal is to buy as prices sometimes tend to trend upwards thereafter. If the price breaks below the −1 standard deviation level, the signal is to sell as prices sometimes tend to trend downwards thereafter. (See Figure 7.5.)

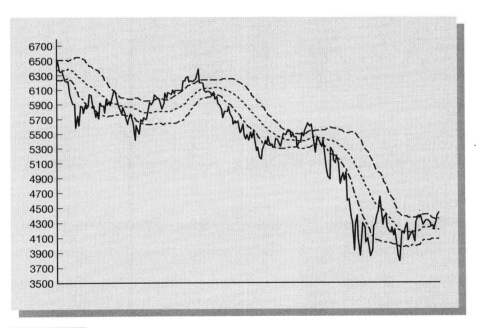

Figure 7.5   **A chart showing the one standard deviation bands**

Notice that prices trend upwards when they are above the upper band and trend downwards when they are below the lower band.

Weaknesses

Volatility breakout systems only work for the market when it is trending. When the market is ranging, the systems generate a lot of false trading signals.

Chapter review

▨ Trading range breakout is a trading strategy to buy when the current price breaks up above a certain trading range and to sell when the current price breaks down below a certain trading range.

▨ The simplest trading range breakout is when the current price moves above the previous x period high or below the previous x period low.

▨ Another way to define trading range is as a constant x% from the moving average. This covers most observations. However, the range area is wide and does not fit the data set well.

▨ A better fit to the data set would be Bollinger bands. These are two standard deviations from the 20-day moving average. Two standard deviations covers 95.5% of all observations in a normal distribution. However, this is not helpful in mechanical trading decision making because two standard deviations define a relative high and low and require other indicators for confirmation.

▨ Therefore, a smaller trading range would be one standard deviation which, if it is a normal distribution, would cover 68% of all observations. A mechanical trading buy or sell signal would occur above +1 or below –1 standard deviations.

▨ The weakness in volatility breakout systems is that they do not work in range trading as they generate a lot of false trading signals.

A NOTE TO THE TRADING APPRENTICE

Size does matter – use the right size moving average!

Note that the shorter moving average has narrower bands and results in quicker/ earlier entry and more whipsaws. This is why the shorter moving average and standard deviation work in a trending market and not in a ranging market.

Note the the longer moving average has broader bands and results in slower entry and fewer whipsaws. This is why a longer moving average and standard deviation work in a ranging market and not in a trending market.

To determine the right size to use, draw several moving average lines. You could try using the Fibonacci numbers, 8, 13, 21 and 34. Select the moving average line that:

▨ generates the least number of whipsaws in a ranging market, and

▨ enters and exits early in a trending market.

In the next chapter, we look at Fibonacci numbers and the waves generated.

8

Wave after wave

What topics are covered in this chapter?

This chapter will discuss the five Elliott waves and their corrections and how these can be measured in Fibonacci ratios. We consider:

■ upward impulse waves

■ downward impulse waves

■ Fibonacci ratios.

What are the objectives?

We need to know about Fibonacci ratios and the concept of waves:

■ To calculate the possibility of potential return versus expected losses (stop loss level).

■ To determine if the risk is worth taking.

Introduction

The patterns on a chart can be seen as waves. A time series can be viewed as a series of wave after wave, and Elliott wave theory is one method of counting waves.[1]

According to Elliott, waves can be measure in multiples and fractions of the Fibonacci golden ratio of 1.618. It is important to know where a wave

---

[1] Elliott wave theory was developed by Ralph Elliott who wrote *The Wave Principle* (1938).

might end as this can give a level to place the stop loss (if the resulting trend is against your position) and a level for projecting possible returns to predict if the risk is worth the reward.

Introduction

Elliott wave theory can be categorised as pattern recognition. The technique here is to identify the wave patterns. Generally, in an impulsive pattern, there are five waves; in a correction pattern, there are three small waves. The waves can be in either direction.

Upward impulse waves

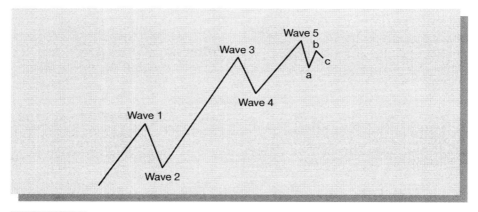

Figure 8.1   **Upward impulse action and its correction**

In an upward impulse action (see Figure 8.1), wave 1 is usually a weak rally with a small number of traders. Wave 2, the counter movement, results from small sell-offs without making a new low. Wave 3 is the huge rally, when the market turns around. Wave 3 starts slowly until it reaches the top of wave 1 where a lot of stops are triggered. Sometimes, there are gap-ups here. After wave 3 has overtaken wave 1, it will rise sharply and quickly as there will be a large number of traders. Wave 3 is the biggest and longest wave. Wave 4 occurs when profit taking sets in. Some traders might see wave 4 as an excellent position to buy after the price has fallen off its high. (However, for experienced traders, wave 4 is generally hard to trade and the potential upside of wave 5 is not worth the risk of

possible further congestion.) Wave 5 is pushed up by this group of traders. Although wave 5 makes a new high above wave 3, interest does not
last and the market tops out. This completes a general five-wave up cycle,
which is usually followed by an a-b-c wave correction as institutional
investors start on their distribution programmes.

Downward impulse waves

In a downward impulse action (see Figure 8.2), wave 1 is usually a weak
distribution phase with a small number of traders. Wave 2, the counter
movement, comes in without making a new high, as retail traders are
trying to get into the market when institutions are selling out. Wave 3
is the huge sell-off, with heavy selling when the market turns around.
At first, the selling is controlled as institutions want to finish their distributions. Wave 3 starts slowly until it reaches the bottom of wave 1
where a lot of stops are triggered. Sometimes, there are gap-downs here.
After wave 3 has fallen below wave 1, it will fall sharply and quickly as
there will be panic selling by the largest number of sellers. Wave 3 is the
biggest and longest wave. Wave 4 occurs when correction sets in. Some
traders might see wave 4 as an excellent position to sell if they were
waiting for a rebound on the way down. (However, for experienced traders, wave 4 is generally hard to trade and the potential downside of wave
5 is not worth the risk of possible further congestion.) Wave 5 is pushed
down by this group of traders. Although wave 5 makes a new low below
wave 3, traders will finally finish their selling and the market bottoms
out. This completes a general five-wave down cycle. This is usually followed by an a-b-c wave correction as institutional investors start on their
accumulation programmes.

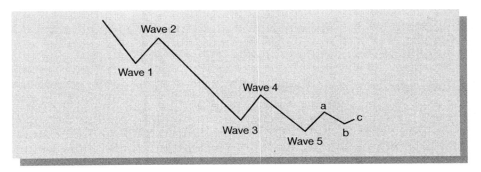

Figure 8.2   Downward impulse action and its correction

General rules for simple impulse and correction waves are as follows:

▓ Wave 2 never retraces back beyond wave 1.

▓ Wave 3 extends beyond wave 1, and is usually the longest and never the shortest.

▓ Wave 4 never retraces beyond wave 3 and usually does not overlap wave 1.

▓ Wave 5 is usually not shorter than wave 1.

Fibonacci ratios and waves

Fibonacci ratios are mathematically derived from the Fibonacci sequence: 1, 1, 2, 3, 5, 8, 13, 21, 34, 55, 89, 144...

The most commonly used Fibonacci ratios in waves are:

▓ in multiples: 1.000, 1.618, 2.618, 4.236

▓ in ratios: 0.236, 0.382, 0.5, 0.618.

For estimating the length of each wave, the following multiples and ratios are used as rough guidelines:

▓ Wave 2 is approximately 0.5 or 0.618 of wave 1.

▓ Wave 3 is approximately 1.618, 2.618 or 4.236 of wave 1.

▓ Wave 4 is approximately 0.236, 0.382 or 0.5 of wave 3.

▓ Wave 5 is approximately 1, 1.618 or 2.618 of wave 1.

Note that these are general guidelines to roughly estimate the height or depth of each wave and cannot be used as strict rules.

Chapter review

▓ Elliott wave theory is used to count wave patterns. Generally, in an impulsive pattern, there are five waves; in a correction pattern, there are three small waves.

▓ Very general rules for the wave count are:

  – Wave 2 never retraces back beyond wave 1.

  – Wave 3 extends beyond wave 1, is usually the longest and never the shortest.

  – Wave 4 never retraces beyond wave 3 and usually does not overlap wave 1.

  – Wave 5 is usually not shorter than wave 1.

▦ The Elliott wave count is based on Fibonacci multiples and ratios of 1.000, 1.618, 2.618, 4.236 and 0.236, 0.382, 0.5, 0.618 respectively.

▦ To estimate the height or depth of each wave, these multiples and ratios are used as rough guidelines:

- Wave 2 is approximately 0.5 or 0.618 of wave 1.

- Wave 3 is approximately 1.618, 2.618 or 4.236 of wave 1.

- Wave 4 is approximately 0.236, 0.382 or 0.5 of wave 3.

- Wave 5 is approximately 1, 1.618 or 2.618 of wave 1.

A NOTE TO THE TRADING APPRENTICE

Believing in waves is dangerous!

Counting waves is OK but believing in what you or others count is dangerous. This is because wave counts are always correct, in exact Fibonacci ratios, only *after* the event. Before the event, the Elliott wave theorist will predict one count up and the alternative count is down. So the probability of the wave count being correct for your trade is only half. Believing in what other theorists count is even more dangerous than your own wave count because even if the theorists have no intention of leading you astray to buy when they are selling (or vice versa) their views might represent what the market mass believes the market will do. And the market usually surprises us.

A last word of caution: let the market pleasantly surprise you but don't let it ruin you. Do not forget to put in place your good-till-cancel (GTC) stop loss order on the alternative Elliott wave count. In other words, if the market does not behave as you have predicted, the alternative wave count is what might occur and where you should put your stop loss. This is why I say that counting waves is fine but believing in them is dangerous (you can be financially ruined). In the next chapter, we relate market phases to waves.

Booms and busts: risks and returns

What topics are covered in this chapter?

In this chapter, we are going to define the most basic cycle in the simplest terms and discuss the risks and rewards associated with buying and selling at each phase of the cycle. We will discuss the reward/risk ratio at:

- the accumulation phase
- the uptrend phase
- the distribution phase
- the downtrend phase.

What are the objectives?

- To determine the appropriate action (buy or sell) at each phase.
- To determine the reward/risk ratio of the action at the phase.

Introduction

There are patterns and trends in the markets. The markets move in cycles as we have seen in the up waves and the down waves. It has been observed time and again that after a period of high, the market drops back to a period of low.

After the big market participants have finished distributing, the market drops back to a low where it then starts accumulating again. The big market players are the professional large financial institutions who usually make money at the expense of small retail players. These large institutions usually make a profit because they buy at market lows and sell higher. They move the market in their direction. The small retail player would do well to know the cycle and follow the direction of the big players.

Introduction

Technical analysis begins with Dow theory. There are two primary movements – bullish primary and bearish primary. The bullish primary begins with accumulation and is followed by an uptrend. The bearish begins with distribution and is followed by a downtrend.

Figure 9.1 shows the four important phases in a cycle. The market is ranging between resistance and support in both the accumulation and distribution periods. It is trending up after breaking above the resistance level and trending down after breaking below the support level.

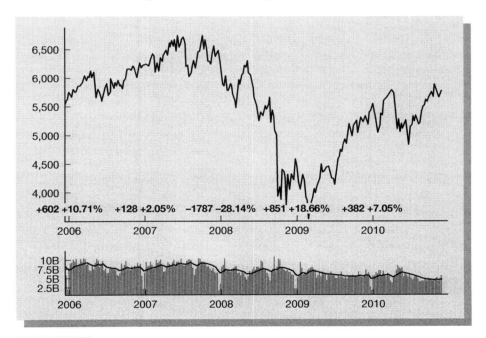

Figure 9.1   Chart showing phases of accumulation, uptrend, distribution and downtrend

Source: From FTSE 100, http://markets.ft.com/markets/interactiveChart.asp

The chart shown in Figure 9.1 begins with a distribution phase from mid-2006 to mid-2008, at between the 5,500 and 6,700 levels. This is followed by the downtrend phase from mid-2008 to the first quarter of 2009, at the 5,500 to 3,700 levels. Accumulation begins from then to the middle of 2009 between the 3,500 and 4,500 levels. An uptrend follows accumulation after breaking out of the 4,500 level until 2010.

When I say distribution (or accumulation), I mean distribution (or accumulation) by the large institutional players who have the ability to move the market in their direction. Some people call this smart money. In order to understand timing the market, we will focus on the main activity of these large market players (or the flow of smart money).

Accumulation phase

Accumulation usually happens near the bottom of a formation, in an area of previous lows. From experience, accumulation of a stock or a basket of stocks takes a few months. The market or the stock would be caught in a certain range between resistance and support, and the moving average line is flattish.

Brokers will not let the stock price go above the agreed resistance by selling aggressively, usually at the end of the day, because they still need to accumulate more stock. In the same way, brokers will not allow the stock price to go below the agreed support by buying aggressively because the lower price will be reflected in a lower value of their stock portfolio and will affect the margin if the stocks were bought on margin. In terms of waves, these scenarios may be counted as the a-b-c wave correction.

In the above example, the accumulation low of around 4,000 is about 0.618 times the distribution high of 6,500. (This so happens to be in proportion to the Fibonacci ratio.)

Uptrend phase

From experience over the past decade, when the smart money has finished accumulating about 80% of its intended holdings in one broking house, it will aggressively buy the remaining 20% at the offer prices, thus pushing the price above the previous resistance using another broking house. This is the range breakout time when your trading system should emit a buy signal. The price should be above the moving average and the moving average line should start to slope upwards. The reward to risk ratio for a long signal is high and the projected level is about 1.618 times the low. Therefore, it is worth risking entering the market.

In the above example, 1.618 times the low is about 6,000. That is 1,500 points from the breakout at 4,500. However, the risk is that it is not a breakout. If the stop loss is placed at 150 points, then the reward to risk ratio (of 10 times) is worth taking.

Distribution phase

Distribution happens after fund managers are satisfied with their profits. From limited experience, this is at least 20% from the average buying price during the accumulation period. The first broker will be selling 80% of stockholdings during the distribution phase.

In the example above, if the initial resistance level where the buying accumulation occurred was around the 4,500 level, then 20% above that or the average buying price would be roughly 5,500. This 5,500 level can then be projected to be a lower range support of this distribution period.

The first broker will not let the stock price go below the agreed support by buying aggressively, usually at the end of the day, because the fund managers still need to distribute more stock. The moving average line is flattish.

In terms of waves, this may be viewed as the a-b-c wave correction.

Downtrend phase

From experience over the past decade, when the smart money has finished distributing about 80% of its holdings, it will use the remaining 20% to keep selling to the bid, pushing the price below the current support. This is the range breakout time when your trading system should emit a sell signal. The price should be below the moving average, and the moving average line should start to slope downwards. The projection level for the move is 0.618 times the high. The reward to risk ratio for a short position is high. Therefore, it is worth risking entering the market.

In the above example, 0.618 times the high is about 4,000. That is 1,500 points from the breakout at 5,500. However, the risk is that it is not a breakout. If the stop loss is placed at 150 points, the reward to risk ratio (of 10 times) is worth taking.

In my experience, downtrends are more fun and easier to capture and play because they happen very fast and you can make fortunes out of them.

Chapter review

■ Technical analysis begins with Dow theory's two primary movements – bullish primary and bearish primary. The important phases are accumulation, uptrend, distribution and downtrend.

■ In the accumulation and distribution periods, the market is ranging between resistance and support. The moving average line is observed to be flattish.

■ The market is in an uptrend if it successfully breaks up above resistance and the technical buy signal appears when the price is above the upward sloping moving average line. The market is in a downtrend if it successfully breaks down below support and the technical sell signal appears when the price is below the downward sloping line.

■ The reward to risk ratio for buying is high when the price first breaks successfully above the range's resistance level in an uptrend because the projection level is 1.618 times off the range's low.

■ The reward to risk ratio for selling is high when the price first breaks successfully below the range's support level in a downtrend because the projection level is 0.618 times off the range's high.

A NOTE TO THE TRADING APPRENTICE

The bull climbs up the stairs but the bear jumps out of the window!

There is a saying: the bull climbs slowly up the stairs but the bear jumps out of the window. So always be alert for the breakdown from the support level of the distribution phase. This can happen if the price closes below the previous low convincingly, your very tight Bollinger bands burst open and the price is below one standard deviation BBZ convincingly.

When there are constant news reports that the economy is booming, prices are going up and taxi drivers are giving you tips on the stock market, be alert for the unexpected. This happens when the Bollinger bands are tightening near the top. If the price breaks out on the downside, sell like mad because the bear is jumping out of the window. These scenarios are usually perpetuated by credit squeeze and margin calls which result in a further downtrend: these are the moments that trend traders like myself are waiting for.

Always be ready to sell because the market falls very fast and steeply. You have to be alert to catch its fall. After that big fall, your fortune is made and your trading career secured forever.

Remember that the four important phases in a cycle are a bullish primary movement that begins with accumulation between support and resistance, followed by breakup to an uptrend. Similarly, the bearish primary movement begins with distribution and is followed by a breakdown into a downtrend. Trend traders are always waiting for breakouts into new trends; both uptrend and downtrend. The downtrend happens faster because fear is greater than greed.

You should be able to see that we are now putting together what we learnt earlier and applying it to trading. From observations of past price movements, we use the theorems of technical analysis to decipher different phases of accumulation, uptrend, distribution and downtrend. We then use technical indicators like moving average to determine the trading signal: that is, to buy when the price is above the moving average and to sell when the price is below the moving average.

The next step is to put these concepts into mathematical trading rules to build a simple mechanical trading system.

10

The secret

What topics are covered in this chapter?

The technical trading system involves technical indicators (simple algorithms) that suit the markets in which traders are trading. These trading algorithms have been researched and tested to have a statistical edge. Inherent in trading systems are risk control mechanisms. All signals are automated.

This chapter will introduce the concepts involved in algorithm trading. The concepts will be explained in greater detail with examples in the second part of the book. The most basic concepts discussed here are:

- trading algorithms
- optimised parameters
- robustness
- high return to low risk
- average gain must far exceed average loss
- no unexpected losses
- ability to avoid whipsaws
- ability to enter new trends early
- ability to automatically adjust
- efficient execution.

What are the objectives?

- To explain the concepts behind trading systems.

Introduction

Trading is not gambling: it is a profession. Professional traders know that trading is not an art but a science. This is their secret involving their trading systems that they are not going to reveal to the public.

Their trading systems are their ticket to making abnormal returns, but returns will not be abnormal if the trading system is used by everyone. This is because trading is a zero sum game. For someone to win, someone has to lose.

The technical trading system basically consists of a set of trading rules selected after a series of tests to generate trading signals. The trading rules consist of algorithms with optimised parameters to indicate trading signals. The trading signal is either to long or to short a contract.

Learning to design an algorithm trading system is one of the first subjects undertaken by an apprentice trader to become a professional market technician working on the model trading desk in a financial institution. The professional market technician trades according to proprietary algorithm trading systems that are not readily available. Most of these models are developed by a trader for his or her own trading use and it is highly unlikely that they will be shared with the public.

Algorithm trading

Algorithm trading is an automated system of signal generations and order executions. It involves the use of algorithms that are robust in automated trading. Risk control in the form of a stop loss order is also inherent in this automated process. As the process is automated, once implemented it does not require or allow for subjective trading decision making, human judgement or interference. The signal generation and stop loss level results from the algorithms that the quantitative analyst programs in. When audited, all trading decisions are accounted for by the algorithms.

1 Trading algorithms

The reason why trading algorithms are preferred in today's proprietary trading desks is that the resulting systems have been rigorously tested and proven to have a statistical edge that generates net positive returns above the passive benchmark buy-and-hold policy.

The quantitative analyst or algorithm quant trader designs, tests and develops the algorithms that automate all trading decisions and executions. They spend most if not all of their time on the design and improvement of algorithm trading systems. The algorithms developed are selected to be the best performers before they are validated and implemented. The algorithms are selected, innovated and intensively tested to suit the markets that these quantitative traders are trading in. Extensive research is conducted to select the algorithms, usually innovated from existing technical indicators like moving average and standard deviation. Backtests and live tests are conducted repeatedly using different contracts and timeframes.

The use of different algorithms in different markets accounts for the difference in profit performance between one quant trading desk and another.

2 Optimised parameters

The parameters for the technical indicators are optimised to suit past, and hopefully future, prices. The parameters are optimised using trading programs that give maximum profit and the least amount of consecutive losses, using the most recent historical data. This exercise is conducted periodically to enable a better fit to the current data.

3 Robustness

Different parameters are used for different markets and timeframes. The parameters generally correlate with the volatility of the markets. In a higher volatility and faster market, a shorter period parameter is used, and vice versa. In a shorter timeframe, such as hourly, a shorter period parameter is used and vice versa.

4 High return to low risk

Algorithm trading is preferred to traditional discretionary trading because not only are all trading decisions objective and quantifiable when audited, but the algorithms are tested to provide a statistical edge: that is, the expectation of positive returns based on backtesting of returns of past data. The backtests must show a net profit after taking into consideration transaction cost and losses.

5 Average gain must far exceed average loss

Algorithms for automated trading are sets of trading rules or combinations of trading rules. These algorithms are often designed to generate automated signals from basic statistical concepts, time series analysis, quantitative methods and probabilities. If the automated trading system's probability of winning trades is equal to that of losing trades, and the average gain far exceeds the average loss (after taking into consideration transaction costs), the net result of this automated trading can only be net profit.

An algorithm trading system is used because historically it has been tested and proven to have an statistical edge in generating positive abnormal returns above the buy-and-hold policy. The use of a well-defined algorithm trading system is very important to the financial institution that has a house proprietary trading operation. The choice and implementation of an algorithm trading system can be the defining factor in determining the financial institution's overall profit or loss for each accounting period.

6 No unexpected losses

The benefit of using an algorithm trading system is that all trading decisions are objective and quantifiable, which means that every trade can be accounted for by the algorithm when audited. This ensures that all trades, profits and losses are systematic, with no drastic, unexpected huge losses compared to paid-up capital. All losses are expected: there is no such thing as unexpected losses.

While a quantitative trader uses an algorithm trading system, the alternative way to trade is via discretionary decision making using either fundamental analysis or chartist technical analysis. Discretionary trading that is not subjected to limited stop loss is not much different from gambling.

An algorithm trading system involves not only signal generation but also stop loss. A stop loss order is automated and there is no allowance for human judgement or interference. Although the primary objective of a defined algorithm trading system is to generate an excess abnormal return, the function of the defined algorithm trading system also helps to prevent uncontrollable large trading losses which may cause the collapse of the financial institution.

7 Ability to avoid whipsaws

The hardest things for trend trading systems to avoid are whipsaws in a range market. Frequent small losses that accumulate in a range market usually wipe away gains from large trend movements. Therefore, the best that trending systems can do in range trading is to do nothing: do not trade or hold on to one side of the position (either long or short) until the trend sets in (either against or for the position). The quant trader has to find an algorithm (formula) that defines when the market is range trading and when it is trend trading.

8 Ability to enter new trends early

When a trend sets in, it is important to get into it early to enjoy the maximum profit rather than waiting for a longer confirmation, by which time short trends in volatile markets would have ended. It is imperative that the quant trader must find the appropriate algorithm that defines when range trading ends and trend trading begins.

9 Ability to automatically adjust

The quant trader must not only find an appropriate algorithm that distinguishes between range trading and trend trading but must also innovate the algorithm to automatically adjust its parameters to suit the two different market conditions. The trading system must be able to adjust its parameters automatically to be longer term in a range market to avoid whipsaws and to be short term in a trend market to enter into new trends early. We will use the remainder of this book to discuss how to parameterise the trading system to suit all trading conditions.

10 Efficient execution

In a professional model trading desk, all trading decisions are automated according to the selected algorithm. As traders, we have to train ourselves to enter an order, ahead of time, as a stop. In a liquid market, there will be a slippage of a tick between the bid and offer. In a non-liquid market, the slippage can be several ticks. This slippage has to be taken into consideration in backtestings. Professionals usually prefer to trade in liquid markets. However, the exceptional trader who wants to use old models to trade in young markets must key in stop limit orders and guard the positions zealously. If the trading system trades frequently, slippage and transaction costs are big problems. Therefore, experienced traders usually choose trading systems that trade infrequently on big trends where slippage and transaction costs are insignificant.

Chapter review

We need a good, flexible, algorithm trend trading system that is robust and has a statistical edge. It should have the following features:

▦ a well-thought-out design that uses appropriate technical analysis tools

▦ parameters that have been tested not only to fit historical price data but that aim to fit future price movements

▦ be robust in any market and any timeframe

▦ have a high return (profit) to low risk (loss) ratio

▦ have a low maximum drawdown with an inherent loss control mechanism

▦ have equal numbers of winning and losing trades and with the average gain higher than the average loss

▦ be able to avoid whipsaws

▦ be able to enter new trends early

▦ be able to adjust or fine tune to suit different market conditions

▦ ensure efficient execution of trades.

A NOTE TO THE TRADING APPRENTICE

You must do something different to make extraordinary profits

Old trading systems do not work as well as they used to in mature markets because other traders know where the buying and selling levels are. So if you want to make extraordinary profits, try to do something different from the crowd. The well-known trading systems seldom work well in mature markets. Some studies have shown that moving average systems used to work in the foreign exchange markets four decades ago but this is no longer the case. So, as the markets mature, we have to find new trading systems like derivatives of averages (the base used in Dow theory) to find profit.

With the completion of this chapter you now possess the essential technical analysis knowledge to proceed beyond the crowd. The concepts in this book have been organised to make them easy to apply. The next part is the fun bit of systematically applying this body of knowledge and the concepts to make a profit.

The next part of this book is the exciting bit about being your own trader but you have to work at building your own trading system.

Trading is a lone profession; it is the complete opposite of the crowd madness that you see in busy trading pits with streams of conflicting information flowing in. If you are one of the crowd, you will, like them, lose money. Some say that only 5% of traders make money, but most, if not all the people I know, make money in the long run. Now is the time to make money, instead of arguing with the random walkers.

Conclusion: leave the random walkers busy with their arguments – the market technicians are busy making money

What topics are covered in this conclusion?

▨ random walk theory

What are the objectives?

▨ To ascertain that prices may not be random and may have trends.

▨ To show that mechanical trading systems, like the moving average procedure for timing purchases and sales, are better than a passive buy-and-hold policy.

Introduction

There is a third school of thought, advocated by academics like Fama (1965), which believes that no investor can achieve excess return above the benchmark return from the buy-and-hold policy based on the knowledge of historical price patterns. Random walk theory generally states that knowing past price history does not help in predicting future prices because, by their nature, prices are a series of random numbers.

Random walk theory

Fama (1965) states in 'Random Walks in Stock Market Prices' that the past history of a series cannot be used to predict the future in any meaningful way and that the future path of a security's price is no more predictable than the path of a series of random numbers. This theory is popularly known as the random walk theory. If this theory is valid, technical and fundamental analyses are completely without value.

The random walk theory, in simple form, can be stated as:

$$P_t = P_{t-1} + \mu_t$$

where P_t is the price at time t, P_{t-1} is the price in the immediately preceding period and μ_t is a random error term.

P_t, P_{t-1} and μ_t are purely random processes, what statisticians call independent and identical distributions, such as a Gaussian normal bell-shaped curve with zero mean. The price change, $\Delta P_t = P_t - P_{t-1}$, is simply μ_t which is not predictable from previous price changes.

Fama (1965) states that the independent price changes assumption of random walk theory is valid as long as knowledge of the past behaviour of a series of price changes cannot be used to increase expected gains. Therefore, he argues that a simple buy-and-hold policy will be as good as any more complicated mechanical procedure for timing purchases and sales.

Fama (1965) suggests testing the hypothesis that successive price changes are independent using at least two different methods:

- testing successive price changes to see whether or not they are independent using a procedure that relies primarily on common statistical tools

- testing directly different mechanical trading rules to see whether or not they provide profits greater than a naïve buy-and-hold policy.

The simplest statistical tool in the first method is to plot the daily price changes over a period of time and check if the histogram forms a normal bell-shaped curve. If the price changes form a sequence of independent and identically distributed random variables, they would spread out in a normal Gaussian distribution. If they do not spread out in a normal bell-shaped curve with zero mean, as in the figure below, then it cannot be inferred that the price series is composed of random variables.

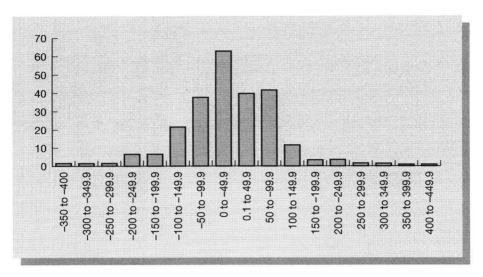

Distribution of daily price changes for the FTSE 100 from 2/1/2008 to 31/12/2008

In the figure above, if you observe the histogram of daily price changes of the FTSE 100, you can see that the distribution is not normal. This means that FTSE 100 price values are not random. This distribution has fat and long tails. To us, this means that there are trends in the FTSE 100 that can be traded on.

Mandelbrot (1963) points out in 'The Variation of Certain Speculative Prices' that there are at least four contradictions to the assumption that successive prices are independent Gaussian random variables:

1   There are more large price changes than predicted by Gaussian.

2   The large price changes seem to be predicted by causal rather than stochastic models.

3   Successive price changes do not look independent but exhibit a number of repeated recognisable patterns.

4   Price records do not look stationary, and sample variances take on very different values at different times.

Mandelbrot (1967), in his experiment with US cotton prices, found that the curve of the price changes is not that of a normal Gaussian distribution but a curve with heavy tails. Mandelbrot and Hudson (2004) state that the variance in US cotton prices gyrates a hundred fold, never settles down to a constant value and is far from being well-behaved and holding steady as the standard Gaussian bell-shaped curve predicts. In fractal geometry, Mandelbrot and Hudson (2004) use power law or scaling, and when applied to cotton prices find an alpha of 1.7. This is not in line with the normal Gaussian distribution's alpha of 2.0.

The second method of testing if prices are random is to test directly different mechanical trading rules to see whether they provide profits greater than a naïve buy-and-hold policy. Many studies have risen to this challenge and several are cited in the bibliography at the end of this book for readers who are interested in empirical studies of the profitability of technical trading rules.

In summary, in studies done by others and myself, most of the technical rules show profits while only a handful show losses and mixed results. These tests are mainly on moving average technical trading systems, equity indices and commodities futures. The conclusion reached is that mechanical technical trading rules generate abnormal returns better than the passive buy-and-hold policy in the long run.

Conclusion review

- Random walk is a theory of the market advocated by academicians like Fama who says that futures prices will be random and no models can predict price movement.

- However, many academic studies like Irwin and Park (2004, 2009) show technical trading models can produce better than passive buy-and-hold returns.

- Some of the trading models that produce abnormal returns are moving average trading systems on futures and equity markets.

A NOTE TO THE TRADING APPRENTICE

Do not be fooled by randomness

Why should we spend time arguing with the random walkers when we can be quietly making profits? Let the professors continue to teach random walk theory in business schools. Why should we bother them in their academic world when we can be making profits in ours? The person who is right in the market is the one who makes money in the long run.

Random walk was what I learnt in school. But in what seems to be randomness, there are repeating patterns. This is what is advocated in fractal geometry theory by the renowned mathematician Benoit Mandelbrot. Our task here is to decipher some of the helpful patterns with professional technical tools to harvest profits in the repeating habits of history.

Let the research analysts do their fundamental research; we do not need it. Fundamental analysis courses have cost me and many others many years of missed profits. This is what I meant when I said, not only do you not need a finance or economics degree to trade, you are much better off without one. You just need to know what the professional traders who are making money in the market know.

You will have realised by now that technical analysis, whether involving subjective pattern recognition or mechanical trading systems, is based on the four concepts of price–volume relationship, trading ranges, trend identification and buy and sell signals that we learnt about earlier. We are building layer upon layer of understanding basic technical analysis so that we can put this knowledge to use with the skills that we will be discussing in the next stage of your development as a savvy, informed market technician.

It is recommended that you adopt the concepts set out in Part 2 before attempting to trade in any market.

Trading with professional technical systems

Introduction: the trading game plan

In the first part, we built a foundation of knowledge of technical analysis for trading. In this second part, we will apply that knowledge to design, build and test trading systems that we can use for our trading.

Model trading is a term used by professional traders for their proprietary trading desks. These traders use proprietary models that are not readily available in the market. It is important to use algorithm trading models because not only are all trades accounted for by the algorithm when audited, but the possibility of financial ruin is theoretically zero. This is due to the inherent stop loss mechanism that is incorporated into the algorithm. In fact, this is the most important criterion that model designers and validators look at when accessing a trading system. The second most important criterion is the track record of previous returns compared with other models in the selected markets.

Most models are developed by the traders themselves for their own trading use and they are not likely to divulge them to the public. This part of the book shares with you the tools and techniques that professional traders use to build their proprietary trading models.

In this part we study in depth the first 10 steps to becoming a professional trader, including:

1 selecting what technical indicators to use

2 designing your own professional algorithm trading system

3 conducting your own data research

4 writing out your trading system using mathematical formulas

5 programming your own mechanical trading system

6 drawing your own trading plan

7 knowing the necessary capital requirements

8 managing risk and losses

9 conducting your own trade evaluation

10 understanding some trading styles.

Below is a flowchart of what we plan to do next in the course of becoming a professional trader.

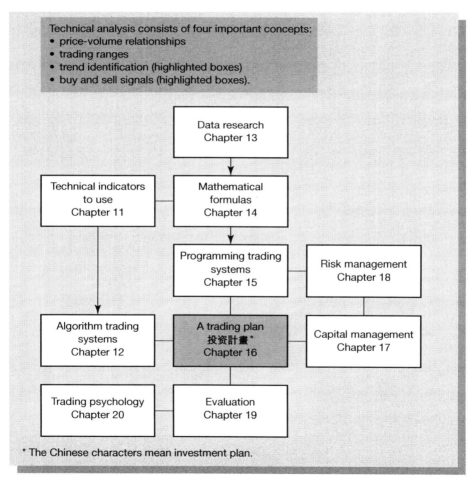

Technical analysis consists of four important concepts:
• price-volume relationships
• trading ranges
• trend identification (highlighted boxes)
• buy and sell signals (highlighted boxes).

Data research
Chapter 13

Technical indicators
to use
Chapter 11

Mathematical
formulas
Chapter 14

Programming trading
systems
Chapter 15

Risk management
Chapter 18

Algorithm trading
systems
Chapter 12

A trading plan
投資計畫 *
Chapter 16

Capital management
Chapter 17

Trading psychology
Chapter 20

Evaluation
Chapter 19

* The Chinese characters mean investment plan.

The layout of Part 2

In the following charts we will learn that all trading decisions must be made on a selected trading system that has been researched and backtested as profitable in the past, in the selected instruments. All buy or sell must be mechanical, based on certain formulas that can be programmed into a trading system. In this agreed trading system and plan, the most important elements are risk or loss management and capital preservation. Evaluation and fine tuning is required periodically in professional trading. Lastly, we will evaluate your trading style to see if you are ready to trade professionally.

The learning objectives of this part are to guide you step-by-step through the phases of research, data analysis, designing and programming your own trading system, writing your own trading plan and trading professionally with risk and loss management, and adequate capital requirements.

We will use very simple, basic statistics, and run backtest and optimisation tests using quantitative methods and simple probability theory. To begin with we will first run through the set-up of the professional trading desk.

Set-up of a professional trading desk

To set up our trading operations, we must learn the functions of a professional model trading desk. This consists of a head of proprietary trading who may also be the designer of the algorithm trading systems and/or who assesses and approves the algorithm trading systems that his or her traders design for different markets. The trader who designs the algorithm trading system is responsible for it, and their individual income is closely tied to its performance. This algorithm trading system must first be validated by the quantitative model validator and approved by the head of proprietary trading who has the authority to set a certain level of acceptable possible loss predicted by the trading system based on past performance. A proprietary model trading desk's checklist would consist of the following (see the figure below):

▩ proprietary trading systems

▩ data analysis and research

▩ track record, backtesting and optimisation

▩ many different markets and trading instruments

▩ different trading techniques

▩ trading rules

▩ live monitoring of positions and risk management

▩ enough capital allocation to capture trend

■ periodic evaluation

■ efficient, unemotional execution.

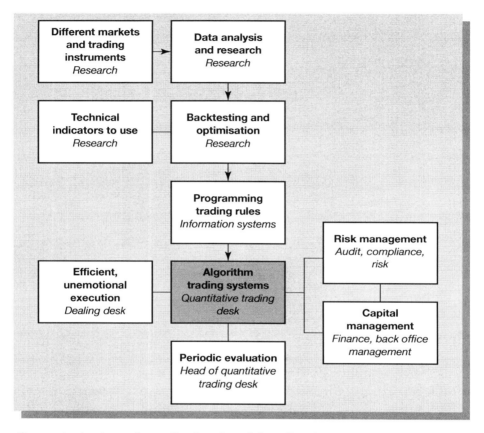

Conceptual set-up of a professional model trading desk

The audit, compliance and risk management departments ensure that the trader executes the trade according to the algorithm trading system that has been approved and the position is accompanied by a trailing stop loss which is decided on entry of the position within the limit of approved loss.

The back office clears the trade and ensures an appropriate margin is maintained for the position with the exchange's clearing house. The position is maintained and the loss (or profit) is monitored live by the risk management department until the position is closed by an offsetting trade. If there is a loss from marked-to-market activity at the end of each trading day, the back office will remit the necessary margin top-up to the clearing house the following day before trading begins. In an integrated system, while the finance department will be immediately alerted to this outflow of funds, management's urgent attention will also be captured if there is any anomaly.

Therefore, when there is any large loss, not just one or two rogue traders are involved but the whole trading desk, the audit, compliance and risk management department, the back office, and the management and the board of directors who agreed to the algorithm trading system. While small, defined losses that may result from this operation are acceptable, it is not possible to generate losses large enough for the attention of the world media if you use an algorithm trading system.

The professional trading desk consists of a mechanical trading system that must be accounted for when audited. What we hope to achieve is to build a technical trading system that has been backtested. Hopefully, this is the system that you will use for your trading.

Writing the rules and building the system may seem like a lot of research and hard work but it is, in fact, the simple part. The harder part is the disciplined act of following the chosen trading system exactly. This is depicted by the dealing desk where dealers execute the orders they receive from traders mechanically and without emotion. Their performance bonuses, if any, will be based on making minimal or no execution mistakes and slippage.

For the trading house, the two functions of trading and dealing are rightly separated and therefore no emotions or egos are involved. For the trader, these two functions are performed by an individual who must therefore follow the trading system exactly, without any emotion or ego.

While this book will help you design and build your trading system, I must stress to the apprentice trader that you must follow your chosen system at all times. This is because the trading system that you have chosen, from among many, has been researched and backtested many times, and will probably have a proven track record.

In fact, the head of a proprietary desk will be looking at potential new traders' track records when they come for interviews for trading positions. The head of model trading will note whether the house is prepared to withstand the maximum consecutive losses that a model can potentially give. Real time, online monitoring of these positions and the risks they represent is absolutely essential. One risk officer might be assigned to be solely responsible for monitoring the positions of the entire house. However, each trader should be responsible for monitoring the stop loss (maximum loss per trade) of his or her own position. Of course, the head of model trading, or the trader him or herself, can readjust the parameters to improve trading performance on a regular basis.

The trading technique here is to have a wide range of investments to choose from to ensure the highest return to risk ratio, to define trend trading from range trading (for it is trend trading that offers the higher return) and to have enough markets to trade as markets do not trend all the time.

Review

▨ The proprietary house business is separated from the agency business.

▨ There are no emotions or egos involved in professional trading (traders get taps on their shoulders and lose their jobs if they do not perform).

▨ Traders are prepared to lose a little in order to win a lot.

A NOTE TO THE TRADING APPRENTICE

Be prepared for small losses and large gains

This is the beginning of your trading experience, to trade using other people's knowledge. With the same concepts, you will soon develop your very own trading system. With a mechanical system, there is no need to 'guesstimate' and feel bad if your position is against you. The bad position will have been cut off early. After a couple of small stop losses, you will accept small losses in your stride as you come to realise that small losses are part of the trading game. How you take losing in trading will determine if you are qualified to be a professional trader.

In trading, you must not only be able to accept the small losses. The more important thing, which most people are not psychologically prepared for, is the enormous gains. Remember, only small losses and large gains will result in net profit.

Most people like to take their profits as soon as they see them without allowing the trend to run its course. They try to re-enter the same trend again much later, usually with losses. If you miss the trend, you will have to wait for another one. That is why you must not exit a big trend too early: exit only at the signal to do so. There are no target prices, levels or profits, just as there are no fortune telling crystal balls. Always remember small losses and small gains will only result in overall losses due to transaction costs.

Generally, the proprietary trading system is a trend-following trading system. A trend trading system is usually mechanical and can be backtested. The most important reason for choosing a trend trading system as the proprietary system is that it generally offers higher returns on risk. In a mechanical trend trading system the losses incurred are limited and small: there is no such thing as a huge loss when using such a system.

The benchmark for any trading system is that it must beat and do better than the passive buy and hold strategy. The following chapter introduces some of the technical indicators used in trading systems.

11

Technical indicators to use

What topics are covered in this chapter?

Inside the black box of trading systems are technical indicators that we can use as trading tools. Some of the popular technical indicators used are:

■ moving averages and standard deviations

■ moving average technique

■ standard deviation bands (BBZ) breakout technique.

However, there are many other indicators designed by different traders that are also in use.

What are the objectives?

The primary aim of this chapter is to provide you with the background knowledge to develop your own trading techniques, which will ultimately be incorporated into your own trading system. We focus on how to use trading tools – technical indicators created by others or created by yourself for your own individual needs to suit a particular market and which may be based on volatilities. The technical indicators are different variations of price and volume.

If a person trades without a trading system and does not have any trading technique, he or she must be using the primal emotions of greed and fear. This commonly results in overtrading, false rumour entries, premature profit taking and holding on to losing trades.

Therefore, the apparent benefit of using systematic techniques that are incorporated into a defined trading system is that all signals generated are mechanical. When trading decisions have been mechanised, the interfering emotions of greed and fear, which consume so many uninformed traders, are removed. The trader can concentrate on improving his or her particular trading system and executing trades accordingly. Consistent execution according to a proven trading system that has been backtested can ensure potential profits. Inherent in this mechanical system is an inbuilt risk control mechanism called stop loss. By consistently practising this early stop loss programme, and by letting profits run their course, the net performance result of a disciplined trader can only be net profit.

It is up to the individual trader to find the model that suits him or her and the markets being traded. The trading model includes factors such as how much risk the trader can tolerate and how much capital he or she is willing to part with.

Introduction

In the first part of the book, we explored and examined some of the popular and useful technical indicators such as moving averages and standard deviations. In this part, we will first learn to apply, then test and fine-tune these indicators to help us profit from the markets. Technical indicators are used in model trading systems because they are mathematically calculated formulas that can result in a totally mechanical execution of buy and sell signals.

Moving average and standard deviation

The trading properties that interest technical analysts are return and risk. In finance theory, average depicts expected return and standard deviation depicts expected risk. In statistics, we can define range trading as prices that are observed within the expected one standard deviation bands. We can also define trend trading as prices that are observed above the plus one (+1) standard deviation band (for an uptrend) and below the minus one (–1) standard deviation band (for a downtrend). We have already identified moving average and standard deviation as tools for this trading technique.

Moving average technique

The best and simplest trading technique is moving average. The basic concept underlying moving average systems is that if the current price is higher than the average price over previous days, there is a possibility of a new uptrend. If the current price is lower than the average price over previous days, there is a possibility of a new downtrend. The technique is to:

▪ buy when the price moves above the moving average (P > MA) and

▪ sell when the price moves below the moving average (P < MA).

Finding the right number (n) of days for the moving average is the key. Generally, you may try the Fibonnaci numbers, 8, 13, 21 and 34. The rule is to select a number that:

▪ results in the least number of whipsaws, and

▪ enters and exits the new trends early.

See Figure 11.1.

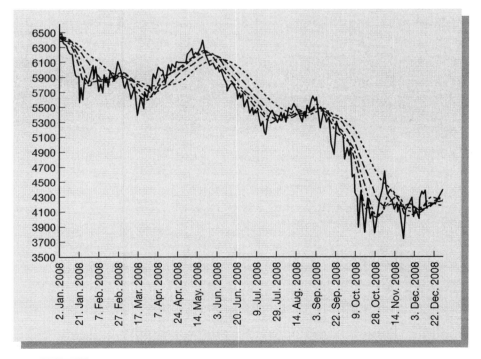

Figure 11.1   Chart showing 8-, 13-, 21- and 34-day moving averages for daily FTSE 100 closing prices

From observation, it can be seen that the 34-day moving average satisfies these two conditions (see Figure 11.2).

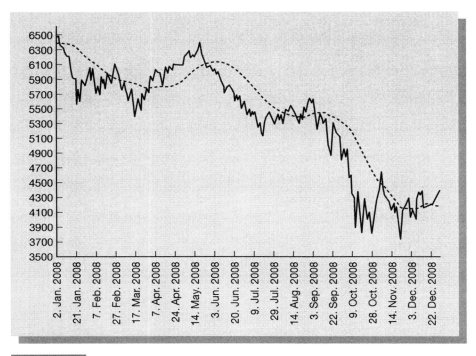

Figure 11.2   **Chart showing 34-day moving average for daily FTSE 100 closing prices**

A profitability test on a 34-day moving average trading technique can confirm whether it is a profitable and thus suitable length moving average to use. Using the simple trading rules of selling below the moving average and buying back above the moving average, this strategy gives a 776 index point gain from 9/9/2008 to 4/11/2008.

Example

▩ **Sell (enter short)** when price was at 5,415.5, **less** than moving average at 5,445.0, on 9/9/2008.

▩ **Buy (exit short)** when price was at 4,639.5, **more** than moving average at 4,506.9 on 4/11/2008.

The profit is 776 index points.

Standard deviation bands (BBZ) breakout technique

The basic concept underlying breakout systems is that if the market makes a new high, there is a possibility of a new uptrend. If the market makes a new low, there is a possibility of a new downtrend.

The standard deviation bands (BBZ) breakout technique is to use the standard deviations from the moving average instead of 10%. If the price breaks above the +1 standard deviation, it is a buy signal. If it breaks below the –1 standard deviation, it is a sell signal. These simple trading techniques can be drafted into what some traders call trading rules:

▨ **Buy (enter long)** when prices are **more** than one standard deviation (P > upper band).

▨ **Sell (exit long)** when prices are **less** than one standard deviation (P < upper band).

▨ **Sell (enter short)** when prices are **less** than minus one (–1) standard deviation (P < lower band).

▨ **Buy (exit short)** when prices are **more** than minus one (–1) standard deviation (P > lower band).

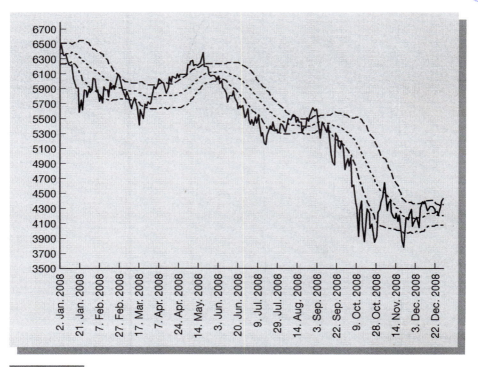

Figure 11.3   Chart showing one standard deviation bands for daily FTSE 100 closing prices

A profitability test on a 34-day standard deviation bands trading technique can be conducted to confirm that it is profitable. Using the simple trading rules of selling below the lower –1 standard deviation band and buying back above the lower –1 standard deviation band, this strategy gives an 846 index points gain from 26/9/2008 to 29/10/2008 (see Figure 11.3). Note that with this technique you enter later than the moving average on more confirmation and exit earlier than the moving average.

Example

▪ **Sell (enter short)** when the price was at 5,088.5 **less** than the –1 standard deviation lower band at 5,158.7 on 26/9/2008.

▪ **Buy (exit short)** when the price was at 4,242.5 **more** than the –1 standard deviation lower band at 4,090.3 on 29/10/2008.

The profit is 846 index points.

Chapter review

▪ Research on the data series must include data analysis on averages and standard deviations. In finance theory, average depicts expected returns and standard deviation depicts risk. Different traders use different techniques. They have different expectations and reward–risk appetites and may use different strategies depending on the amount of capital and risk/loss tolerance.

▪ The moving average trading technique employs the concept of going long when prices are above the moving average and going short when prices are below the moving average.

▪ The volatility breakout trading technique called BBZ employs the concept of going long when prices are above +1 standard deviation and going short when prices are below –1 standard deviation.

A NOTE TO THE TRADING APPRENTICE

The right order

Using your trading system, enter and exit the market immediately and mechanically at the signals to do so. The right technique for executing orders is to sell to the bidder or buy from the seller at the best available market price. This is to prevent missing the price because when the market trends, prices tend to run away. Some novice traders have tried to place limit orders to buy lower than the market price or sell higher than the market price only to find that the market never retraces to give them a chance to enter their positions, and prices have run away in the direction of their signals. The advice here is to forget the few points that can be gained from placing limit orders that are better than the market price. Trade at market prices because when trend signals come, the chances are high that prices will continue trending further away in the direction of the signals.

More important than placing market orders is placing a good-till-cancel (GTC) stop loss order at the point of entry. This is to prevent overloss. It is human nature to avoid losses. An automated GTC stop order at the point of entry eliminates the pain of cutting your loss at the pre-determined cut loss level. This is the professional thing to do because the expected loss can be imputed into the calculation of the risk to reward ratio. This is an important part of the trading plan.

To beat the general market masses, some adjustments may be necessary to change these very common techniques into something extraordinary that is suited to trading in your particular market. This adaptation to a local market requires some research into the properties of the price series being traded. After research, fine tuning of the number of periods for the moving average or standard deviation is required. A shorter number of periods will catch the trend earlier but will result in a lot more false trades in range trading. A longer number of periods will miss out a larger part of the trend's initial movement but is more confirmed.

12

Principles of a technical algorithm trading system

What topics are covered in this chapter?

This chapter shares insider concepts of how to build successful algorithm trading systems for profitable trading. It researches the concepts that form the technical indicators and techniques that professional market technicians use to build their proprietary trading models. The topics discussed are:

- addressing the most common problems of trend trading systems
- profile of an algorithm trend trading system.

What are the objectives?

Learning to design an algorithm trading system is one of the first subjects undertaken by an apprentice trader in order to become a professional market technician working on the model trading desk in a financial institution. The professional market technician trades according to proprietary algorithm trading systems that are not readily available in the market. Most of these models are developed by the trader for his or her own trading use.

Introduction

The most general principle of algorithmic trading (also known as automated, algo, black box or robo trading) is finding an algorithm that is suitable to the prevailing market condition and automatically executing the trading signal via a computer program. The algorithm is selected after intensive backtesting and optimisation. An algorithm trading system is used because historically it has been tested and proven to have a statistical edge in generating positive abnormal returns above the buy-and-hold policy.

Addressing some common problems in trend trading systems

All trading systems have problems. Trend trading systems have problems that are specific to them:

▪ There are too many similar trend trading systems that generate similar kinds of orders, thus creating false signals when there are no real trends.

▪ Trend trading systems suffer whipsaws when the market is ranging.

▪ The fast trend trading systems tend to exit the market too early and thus do not capture most of the major price movements.

▪ The slow trend trading systems fail to enter the market early and miss large portions of major price movements, especially when prices move unexpectedly and sharply.

▪ Most of the time, the trading system parameters have to be fine-tuned to meet current market conditions.

BBZ aims to address the five most common problems inherent in trend trading systems.

1 **There are too many similar trading systems.** As BBZ is an original and not widely known trading system, it does not generate many false trading signals triggered by similar orders from other common standard trading systems.

2 **Trend trading systems generate too many whipsaws.** BBZ experiences fewer whipsaws than most trading systems because it adapts to market conditions and has been designed to avoid as many whipsaws as possible in a range market.

3 **Fast trend trading systems do not capture large portions of major price movements.** Unlike some trend trading systems that exit too early and miss out on additional profit, BBZ rides on the trend from the time the signal emerges on expansion of the bands until the exit signal at the contraction of the bands. The risk of BBZ exiting too early is low as it adapts to the prevailing market conditions. Should BBZ exit falsely, it will re-enter at the original position on the signal to do so.

4 The slow trading systems tend to give up a large portion of potential profits. BBZ can be optimised to enter and exit earlier on a change of trend.

5 The trend trading systems do not change according to market conditions. BBZ can be optimised to change the parameters (moving averages and standard deviations) according to market conditions. Use a long-term moving average and standard deviation in a range market and a short-term moving average and standard deviation in a trend market.

To sum up, the most important feature of an algorithm trading system is its ability to adapt quickly and be robust in all markets and across time. In designing a new algorithm trading system, the technical indicator used should show this ability.

Profile of an algorithm trend trading system

According to Chande (1997), a trading system is used to gain a statistical edge, objectivity and consistency. The trading system must be robust. A robust trading system is defined as one that can withstand a variety of market conditions across many markets and timeframes. The trader can trade in timeframes of seconds, minutes (five, 10, 15, 30), hourly, daily and weekly. It is rare to find a trader who uses a monthly or yearly timeframe because trends happen within the month and the majority of the profit would have been missed on monthly confirmation.

Two market conditions that are important to traders are:

■ a range market when there is little price movement, which results in small gains for the range trader and small losses for the trend trader

■ a trend market when there is a large price movement, which results in huge gains for the trend trader and huge losses for the range trader.

Therefore, generally most traders would prefer trading in a trend market.

The trading system must be backtested and tested live (in line with out-of-sample testing) to withstand these two very different market conditions and the results of these tests must be positive. As Chande (1997) puts it, the trading system must have a positive expectation. He also states that the most important reason to use a trading system is to gain a statistical edge. This statistical edge also refers to the probability of ruin. The smaller the probability of ruin, the more likely the trader survives and profits from the trading system in the long run.

A good, flexible, algorithm trend trading system that is robust and has a statistical edge should aim to be tested according to the following criteria:

1 A well thought out design that uses appropriate technical analysis tools

As we have seen earlier, lagging indicators like moving average and standard deviation have an advantage as they are mean reverting. This means that the potential stop loss, if placed at the moving average or standard deviation levels, is relatively small. This is part of the reason why we have selected moving average and standard deviation as tools to be incorporated into our trading system.

2 Parameters that have been tested not only to fit historical price data but that aim to fit future price movements

Selecting a parameter based on historical data is easy, because optimisation tests are simple to do with a computer program. It is a matter of choosing the highest net profit at the lowest maximum consecutive loss. To fit future price movements we are making the assumption that present and future movements will be like those of the past. This may or may not be true. If it is not true, we need to do some fine tuning. Therefore, it is better if the trading program incorporates an algorithm that performs this fine tuning or optimisation automatically.

3 Ability to be robust in any market and any timeframe

A good trading system is robust across most markets. A trend trading system tends to do better with daily data but in fast, volatile markets a daytrader may apply the trading system after rigorous testing. The futures markets that we have used to test our trading system are Nikkei, SPI, KOSPI, SiMSCI, Hang Seng, FKLI, FCPO, soyoil, soybean and corn futures.

4 High profits to low risk ratios

The total accumulated profits net of all transaction costs compared with the total accumulated losses of the trading system give this reward to risk ratio. The higher this ratio, the better the trading system is. As a rule of thumb, this ratio should be at the very least more than 1.5.

5 Number of winning trades that are about equal to, or more than, losing trades

Over the long run, on average at any point in time there is a 50% chance that the price will go up and a 50% chance that it will go down. At the point of entry, the chance of the trade being a winning trade is also 50%.

So, if on average, the number of winning trades that the trading system generates is 50%, this should be good enough.

6 Average gain is much larger than average loss

If the chances of winning and losing are the same, the determining factor must be the winning amount. The average gain must be at least 1.5 times larger than the average loss.

7 Capital preservation and low maximum drawdown with an inherent loss control mechanism

The level of drawdown, the maximum consecutive losses that affect the level of capital, determines if an individual can make it as a professional trader. The loss control mechanism is simply a stop loss order. According to the trading plan, the stop loss level must be placed at about one-third of the potential reward. Technically, the stop loss level must be placed at a point where it will not be triggered unnecessarily. Try to place your stop at uncommon areas where the flood of similar orders will not trigger your stop unnecessarily before the market continues to move in the direction of your position.

8 Ability to avoid some of the whipsaws in a range trading market

Trend trading systems share the common problem of suffering whipsaws in a ranging market. The challenge here is to build an algorithm trading system that can avoid some of the whipsaws in a range trading market. We propose widening the trading bands during range trading to avoid some of these whipsaws.

9 Ability to enter a new trend early

A tighter band will allow earlier entry. We propose tightening the trading bands when the market starts to trend.

10 Ability to automatically adjust or fine tune to trend versus range market conditions

The trading system must incorporate an algorithm that automatically adjusts the bands to tighten when the market starts to trend and widen during range market conditions.

The net profit, the number of winning to losing trader and the average gain/average loss for the BBZ trading system and the FTSE 100 is as follows:

Example   BBZ Trading System

Instrument	FTSE 100
Period	2/1/2008–31/12/2008
Buy-hold	–2,023
Net profit/loss	+603
Number of winning trades	6
Number of losing trades	13
Average gain/average loss	3.42

Chapter review

The newly designed algorithm trading system, BBZ, should ideally possess all the above characteristics:

▦ Uses moving average and standard deviation technical indicators.

▦ Has adaptive parameters to fit historical and current data.

▦ Is able to be robust in daily, hourly and half hourly timeframes for futures contracts.

▦ Has a return to risk ratio of at least 1.5.

▦ The number of profitable to unprofitable trades is 50:50.

▦ The average gain is at least 1.5 times larger than the average loss.

▦ Has capital preservation and a low maximum drawdown with an inherent loss control mechanism due to the adaptive nature of moving average and standard deviation.

▦ Is able to avoid some of the whipsaws in a range trading market due to the long-term moving average and standard deviation.

▦ Is able to enter a new trend early due to the short-term moving average and standard deviation.

▦ Automatically adjusts/fine tunes to trend versus range market conditions.

Chande (1997) notes that the average trade profit is supposed to be large enough to make the chosen trading system worth trading. It should cover transaction costs and slippage and should, on average, perform better than competing trading systems.

A NOTE TO THE TRADING APPRENTICE

The black box

This is the black box that I told you fund managers are trying to sell to unsuspecting investors. They ask for your funds to place them in algorithm trading and although they promise good annual returns, the chances are that the good returns will not be what you expect. Is it not time for you to have fun trading your own hard earned funds?

Model black box trading is simple and emotionless: you just follow the proven trading rules. The risks and losses are defined and controllable. The foreseen known dangers are: expected slippage, that is orders being filled at a price worse than the trigger price; and prices whipsawing. However, with defined stop loss, the risks are not high compared to the loss of your entire trading capital.

Trading without a system is dangerous. It is like gambling and the odds are not in the gambler's favour. Trading with a proven system means building your trading business for long-term success. Trading with a stop loss system should never result in any overloss. Overloss is a word synonymous with overtrading and not daring to cut a worsening position in time. Overloss is a word not found in a trading system's dictionary.

To find a proven trading system, you need to know the market's peculiar behaviours. Market statistics will give hints as to the market's characteristics and the trading models that can decipher prominent trends. The next chapter discusses how to find suitable markets and market products.

13

Understanding market characteristics and what to do

What topics are covered in this chapter?

This chapter explores the characteristics of the markets and products, especially futures, which are traded on margin. It covers:

- research characteristics
- research markets
- research product – futures.

What are the objectives?

- The purpose of data analysis is to study the theoretical and empirical properties of the price behaviour of different markets.
- The objective of data analysis is to find the most lucrative markets and products to trade.
- The aim here is to develop the most suitable and effective technical trading system to harvest the maximum profit from the most lucrative markets.

Introduction

This book places a strong emphasis on the theoretical and empirical properties of a time series with the objective of applying the evidence and results to develop and test trading systems that yield high returns at low, controlled risks.

Research characteristics

Before you trade in any market, you must do your own research. In research, the first step is to perform data analysis and know basic statistics such as the averages and standard deviations for returns, prices and volumes.

To determine if the market is in a range or in a trend, look at the moving average. The market is trading in a range if the moving average line is flat and prices whipsaw around it. The market is in an uptrend if the moving average line is upward sloping and prices are above it. The market is in a downtrend if the moving average line is downward sloping and prices are below it.

To determine if a trend is likely to begin, look at the width of the standard deviation bands. The bands usually widen when the trend begins to set in. Therefore, look for unusually narrow bands that look like they may burst open. The finance behaviour explanation is that prices are kept low within range for the accumulation (distribution) to complete and now that the accumulation (distribution) is complete, the price can be bid up (sold down) for the large fund portfolio to experience asset appreciation (to accumulate back at a lower price).

Research markets

Different markets will have different characteristics. So record any observations that you may find about the market, such as the duration of the accumulation and distribution periods. Different products have different levels of risks and returns.

The different markets are the foreign exchange, equity, commodity and futures markets. My literature review shows that currencies appear to be the most popular studies, possibly because they make the most returns. Most of the studies conclude that the trading experience with currencies is positive. Park and Irwin (2004) noted that, in general, technical trading strategies for currencies were profitable until the early 1990s but have not been since then. Stock markets appear to be the second most popular study. Interestingly, Dow Jones Industrial Average stocks, which were profitable earlier, failed to make as many profits after 1990 and new emerging markets show greater potential for profit making using common technical analysis tools like moving averages. Futures markets appear to be least researched. Most of the studies appear to show consistent profits across most of the indices and commodities futures.

Generally, studies show that profits are less in sophisticated and mature markets such as foreign exchange and the stock exchanges of major financial centres. Therefore, research should focus more on less-developed financial markets.

Table 13.1 shows a list of developed and less-developed financial markets and the test results of different trading systems like simple moving average (SMA), moving average crossover (MA Cross), BBZ and optimised BBZ (Opt BBZ) for the year 2008. You can see that the more mature the contract (e.g. DJ Futures), the harder it is to make a profit using a simple known technique and daily closing prices. This is partly because mature markets with their sophisticated players are moving very fast – too fast for the simple moving average to capture using daily prices.

Table 13.1 Test results for trading systems: 2/1/2008–31/12/2008

Contract	Buy & Hold	SMA	MA Cross	BBZ	Opt BBZ
Nikkei Futures	−5940	1155	2385	−250	1625 (33, 1.2)
SPI Futures	−2585	−592	211	−1074	406 (30, 1.1)
KOSPI Futures	−95.1	11.55	37.75	14.65	55.6 (33, 0.8)
SiMSCI Futures	−203.2	44.2	86.6	−56	64.6 (33, 0.8)
Hang Seng Futures	−13263	9151	9297	−131	7877 (29, 0.9)
DJ Futures	−4595	−3535	−2099	−4435	−1292 (28, 1.1)
FTSE 100 Futures	−2023	201	739.5	603.3	673.5 (34, 0.6)
FKLI Futures	−562	433.5	378	213.5	366 (34, 0.8)
FCPO Futures	−1387	820	1719	697	1119 (17, 0.9)
Soyoil	−16.49	19.69	29.22	14.1	27.00 (19, 0.8)
Soybean	−234	540.8	558.2	15.2	522 (9, 1.2)
Corn	−49.2	134.6	52.8	121	328 (26, 0.9)

For illustration purposes, we will use a FTSE 100 futures contract traded on LIFFE-NYSE because it is a popularly traded contract. However, note that profits are hard to find in contracts like this using simple moving averages.

Research product – futures

Exchange traded futures involve a standard contract to buy or sell a specific underlying asset, whether this is a theoretical basket of stocks or a fixed amount of a commodity such as coffee, some time in the future. Futures contracts are standardised according to contract specifications which include:

▦ the underlying asset

▦ the contract value and minimum tick

▦ the contract months and expiry dates

▦ cash settlement or cash delivery.

For example, the contract specifications of a FTSE 100 futures contract traded on NYSE Liffe London are:

▦ The underlying asset is the FTSE 100 Index.

▦ The contract value is £10 per index point with a minimum tick of 0.5 (£5).

▦ The contract months are March, June, September and December with the expiry dates on the third Friday of the contract month.

▦ Cash settlement is according to the exchange settlement price based on an algorithm using the underlying FTSE 100.

Example

Using the BBZ trading system, if on 26/9/2010, we sell one FTSE 100 Dec10 futures contract on the NYSE-Liffe at 5,088.5, and later on 29/10/2010, we buy back one FTSE 100 Dec10 futures contract at 4,242.5 to close, our trading gain is 846.

Our profit before transaction costs is 846 × £10 = £8,460.

Leverage

Futures are traded on margins, which means you do not have to pay for the whole amount of the basket of stocks. You only need to deposit, as margin, a small percentage of the whole contract size. The margin of most futures ranges between 5% and 20% of contract size, based on the clearing house's calculation of the volatility of historical prices.

If the contract value of one FTSE 100 Jun10 futures contract is 5,088.5 × £10 = £50,885, and the margin is £4,105, we only deposit with the futures broker (and the clearing house of the exchange) 8% of the actual contract size.

If our profit before transaction costs is 846 × £10 = £8,460 and the margin paid is £4,105, the return is 206% compared to a return of 16% if you had to pay up the entire contract value or had bought an equivalent value of FTSE 100 basket of stocks.

Futures are highly leveraged and can greatly enhance your portfolio if they are profitable. They can cause financial ruin if the transaction results in great loss. This can be why some people regard futures as a dangerous financial instrument. Professional traders regard futures as one of the best instruments to trade because of very high returns.

FTSE 100 statistics

The first step is to specify the contract to be tested. FTSE 100 is chosen here. To get a feel for the data, the average and the standard deviation for the whole data set is calculated. Usually, the return (current day's close – previous day's close) is used to check the average. Then the standard deviation of the return is calculated to assess by how much the return can deviate from the mean.

The next step is to determine where to get the data. We obtained our data, the daily close of the FTSE 100, from data vendors such as the Financial Times website. (The code is 'FTSE' for FTSE 100.) We will use 250 sample data (see Table 13.2).

Table 13.2 FTSE 100 statistics

Return	Mean	Standard deviation
FTSE 100 Return	−7.99	113.12

This means that the mean daily return of the FTSE 100 for the year 2008 is slightly negative and the daily movement is generally two-thirds of the time within the range of −121 to +105 (if the distribution curve is a normal Gaussian bell shaped curve).

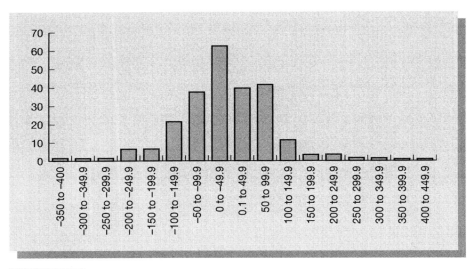

Figure 13.1 **Distribution of daily returns for the FTSE 100:**
2/1/2008–31/12/2008

If you observe the histogram of daily returns of the FTSE 100, you can see that the distribution is not normal and means that FTSE 100 price values are not random. This distribution has fat and long tails so there are trends in the FTSE 100 that can be traded on (see Figure 13.1).

Exercise

1 In http://markets.ft.com/markets/tearsheets/performance, click on 'Historic Prices'.

2 Follow the instructions in the spreadsheet.

3 Paste the copied data onto a worksheet.

4 Calculate the return of close by subtracting the current day's close from the previous day's close [=B3–B2].

5 Calculate the average of the returns by summing all the returns divided by the number of observations [=AVERAGE(C2:C250)].

6 Calculate the standard deviation of the returns [=STDEV(C2:C250)].

Chapter review

▦ Research and trading are the only way you can know your markets well. I don't mean research from newspapers, I mean statistical research that you do yourself. The trading apprentice must know the average of daily returns for the past month versus daily standard deviation to know how prices behaved in the previous month.

▦ Futures markets are the least researched and best markets to trade in terms of directional volatility. Part of the attractiveness of futures relates to the leveraging factor. Futures are traded on small margins.

▦ The return distribution of a price series is generally not a normal distribution: it generally has fat tails. Therefore, the price series is not random but has a trending pattern.

A NOTE TO THE TRADING APPRENTICE

You need a positive statistical expectation edge

Research is the only way to find your positive statistical expectation edge. It is as simple as finding the average daily return and daily standard deviation within a month, a quarter or a year, similar to checking for fat tail distributions. The fatter the tails, the bigger the potential profits and the more lucrative the markets for you to trade.

Futures are one of the best markets to trade because of the leverage factor. Mature markets are more difficult to trade because they are already saturated with sophisticated program trading. Therefore, look for young emerging markets that have simple directional trends. The soft commodities futures markets of the past decade seem to have this feature.

Remember: before you trade, do your own research. I am only pointing the way. You must sit down and find your own statistical positive expectation in the market that you wish to trade in.

Now that you have laid the foundation for your trading we will proceed to building the rest of your trading structure.

14

Simple formulas to design your own trading models

What topics are covered in this chapter?

The trading rules for trading systems are all expressed mathematically. The trading rules for moving average and standard deviation bands, BBZ, are expressed by:

- mathematical formulas in spreadsheets.

What are the objectives?

By having an objective mathematical trading decision process, any trader who possesses the same formula will produce the same result. In this way, a trading journal can be easily audited. The other more important reason for having mathematical formulas is to check for accuracy and correctness when backtesting and in data optimisation.

Introduction

A professional proprietary trading model is usually a mechanical trend trading system that uses mathematical formulas as a base. In this way, all trading decisions are mathematically derived and automated. When audited, all trading decisions can be accounted for.

Mathematical formulas in spreadsheets

By putting mathematical formulas into the spreadsheet, we can calculate the moving average, the standard deviation and finally the Z-test statistic. By calculating these statistics, we can observe if the moving average is not moving, i.e. is flattish, the standard deviation is expanding or narrowing, and finally the Z-test statistic is above +1 or below –1. We can eyeball the data and then do some fine tuning as the chief of a dealing desk would do.

We can count the number of occurrences when the Z-test statistic is between +1 and –1. If prices are random, about 68% of the population should be within +1 and –1 of the standard Z-test, about 15.5% of the population should be above +1 of the standard Z-test and about 15.5% of the population should be below –1 of the standard Z-test. However, when looking at the FTSE 100 sample, we see that about 50% of the sample is within +1 and –1 of the standard Z-test, about 25% of the sample is above +1 of the standard Z-test and about 25% of the sample is below –1 of the standard Z-test. This means that the FTSE 100 sample has a fat tail distribution. A fat tail distribution means that prices tend to trend.

If we are using a simple moving average, the written form of the simple moving average model is:

▓ buy when the price is above the X period moving average

▓ sell when the price is below the X period moving average.

If we are using BBZ, the written form of this model is:

▓ Buy long when the price is above the +1 standard deviation band.

▓ Sell to exit long when the price is below the +1 standard deviation band.

▓ Sell short when the price is below the –1 standard deviation band.

▓ Buy to exit short when the price is above the –1 standard deviation band.

To write out the formulas on the excel spreadsheet, enter in:

```
Column A:  Date
Column B:  Close
Column C:  Moving Average       [=average(B2:B22)]
Column D:  Standard Deviation   [=stdev(B2:B22)]
Column E:  Upper Band           [=C2+D2]
Column F:  Lower Band           [=C2-D2]
Column G:  Buy Signal           [If Column B> Column E, "LONG",
                                " ")
Column H:  Sell Signal          [If Column B< Column F, "SHORT",
                                " "]
```

The calculation of the upper and lower band to determine a long or short position is shown in Table 14.1.

Table 14.1 Calculation of the upper and lower band to determine a long or short position

Date	Close	MA	Stdev	Upper band	Lower band	Long	Short
26/09/08	5088.5	5356.1	197.4	5553.5	5158.7		Short
29/09/08	4818.8	5334.9	215.0	5549.8	5119.9		Short
30/09/08	4902.5	5316.3	224.3	5540.6	5092.0		Short
01/10/08	4959.6	5301.9	231.1	5533.0	5070.8		Short
02/10/08	4870.3	5283.4	239.9	5523.4	5043.5		Short
03/10/08	4980.3	5269.5	243.4	5512.9	5026.1		Short
06/10/08	4589.2	5244.2	267.6	5511.8	4976.5		Short
07/10/08	4605.2	5223.1	288.7	5511.9	4934.4		Short
08/10/08	4366.7	5193.6	322.5	5516.1	4871.0		Short
09/10/08	4313.8	5162.5	354.3	5516.8	4808.2		Short
10/10/08	3932.1	5116.2	407.0	5523.2	4709.2		Short
13/10/08	4256.9	5080.5	427.7	5508.2	4652.9		Short
14/10/08	4394.2	5047.2	435.8	5483.0	4611.3		Short
15/10/08	4079.6	5002.4	454.9	5457.3	4547.5		Short
16/10/08	3861.4	4950.2	481.0	5431.2	4469.2		Short
17/10/08	4063	4904.9	490.1	5395.1	4414.8		Short
20/10/08	4282.7	4865.6	484.6	5350.2	4380.9		Short
21/10/08	4229.7	4828.2	483.2	5311.4	4345.0		Short
22/10/08	4040.9	4789.3	492.0	5281.4	4297.3		Short
23/10/08	4087.8	4755.4	499.6	5255.1	4255.8		Short
24/10/08	3883.4	4709.5	506.0	5215.5	4203.5		Short
27/10/08	3852.6	4663.5	510.9	5174.4	4152.6		Short
28/10/08	3926.4	4621.2	510.5	5131.7	4110.6		Short
29/10/08	4242.5	4589.5	499.2	5088.7	4090.3		

Alternatively, we can calculate the Z-test statistic:

$$Z = \frac{\text{Close} - \text{Moving average}}{\text{Standard deviation}}$$

▪ If (Close – Moving average) > +1 standard deviation, or Z > +1, then it is a "BUY" enter long signal.
▪ The "**SELL**" exit long signal will be when Z < +1.

And:

▪ If (Close – Moving average) < –1 standard deviation, or Z < –1, then it is a "SELL" enter short signal.
▪ The "**BUY**" exit short signal will be when Z > –1.

Enter in:

```
Column A:      Date
Column B:      Close
Column C:      Moving Average [=average(B2:B22)]
Column D:      Standard Deviation [=stdev(B2:B22)]
Column E:      Z Test Statistic [=(B2-C2)/D2]
Column F:      Buy Signal [If B2>1, "LONG", " ")
Column G:      Sell Signal [ If B2<-1,"SHORT", " "]
```

The calculation of the Z-test statistic to determine a long or short position is shown in Table 14.2.

Table 14.2 Calculation of the Z-test statistic to determine long or short position

Date	Close	MA	Stdev	Z-test statistic	Long	Short
26/09/08	5088.5	5356.1	197.4	–1.4		Short
29/09/08	4818.8	5334.9	215.0	–2.4		Short
30/09/08	4902.5	5316.3	224.3	–1.8		Short
01/10/08	4959.6	5301.9	231.1	–1.5		Short
02/10/08	4870.3	5283.4	239.9	–1.7		Short
03/10/08	4980.3	5269.5	243.4	–1.2		Short
06/10/08	4589.2	5244.2	267.6	–2.4		Short
07/10/08	4605.2	5223.1	288.7	–2.1		Short
08/10/08	4366.7	5193.6	322.5	–2.6		Short
09/10/08	4313.8	5162.5	354.3	–2.4		Short
10/10/08	3932.1	5116.2	407.0	–2.9		Short

Date	Close	MA	Stdev	Z-test statistic	Long	Short
13/10/08	4256.9	5080.5	427.7	−1.9		Short
14/10/08	4394.2	5047.2	435.8	−1.5		Short
15/10/08	4079.6	5002.4	454.9	−2.0		Short
16/10/08	3861.4	4950.2	481.0	−2.3		Short
17/10/08	4063.0	4904.9	490.1	−1.7		Short
20/10/08	4282.7	4865.6	484.6	−1.2		Short
21/10/08	4229.7	4828.2	483.2	−1.2		Short
22/10/08	4040.9	4789.3	492.0	−1.5		Short
23/10/08	4087.8	4755.4	499.6	−1.3		Short
24/10/08	3883.4	4709.5	506.0	−1.6		Short
27/10/08	3852.6	4663.5	510.9	−1.6		Short
28/10/08	3926.4	4621.2	510.5	−1.4		Short
29/10/08	4242.5	4589.5	499.2	−0.7		

Example

On 26/9/08, the close is 5,088.5, the moving average is 5,356.1 and the standard deviation is 197.4. The Z-test statistic is (5,088.5 − 5,356.1)/197.4= −1.4. Therefore the signal is short.

On 29/10/08, the close is 4,242.5, the moving average is 4,589.5 and the standard deviation is 499.2. The Z-test statistic is (4,242.5 − 4,589.5)/499.2= −0.7. Therefore there is no longer any signal.

Chapter review

■ A mathematical trading system is usually chosen as the proprietary trading model because all trading decisions are automated.

■ With mathematical formulas, it is easier to check backtesting and optimisation results.

■ It is easy to write mathematical formulas in spreadsheets. Z-test statistics can be calculated as (Close − Moving average)/Standard deviation.

A NOTE TO THE TRADING APPRENTICE

Eyeballing the future

Spreadsheets are very useful in trading system modelling. Besides giving the added advantage of visually seeing the direction of the moving average in numbers, they show whether the bands are expanding or narrowing. Expanding bands mean that trends might be developing.

Spreadsheets are used in the eyeballing process of each trade. Eyeballing is a process of reviewing past price data in relation to the technical indicator for the purpose of making any adjustments necessary to avoid as many false trades as possible while capturing the big trends as early as possible. Some confirmation conditions may also be added into the mechanical system to reduce the number of false signals. Volume and open position are good confirmation signals because they are not derived from price.

In a trading house, this eyeball review is usually conducted by the chief dealer and the trading system designer to check if the system can be further improved. He or she may see a slight change in the parameter(s) resulting in more profits. This parameter change can be implemented in the next period.

We start by writing the mathematical formulas in the spreadsheet before we write the trading program. The trading program will simplify the trader's job by backtesting in a flash. It can also compute optimisations, a task that is almost impossible for the trader to do manually.

15

Programming trading rules into your system

What topics are covered in this chapter?

Writing the trading rules is the simple first step and programming is easy once you know how. Testing and simulations are all part of the practice. Analysing the results and fine tuning the trading system will be discussed in this chapter but the hardest part is to follow the trading signals they generate without emotion and deviation. So here we look at:

- simple moving average trading rules
- BBZ trading rules
- reading and analysing test results.

What are the objectives?

The obvious objective of having a trading system is to make life simple and trading accountable. A trading system is the only professional way to go about trading. Before you start trading any market, a trading system will backtest the historical prices and give you valuable information about the market, which you can use for your projections and trading strategy.

Introduction

A trading system consists of trading rules. Most of the trading rules are very simple. We begin by writing out the trading rules on a piece of paper, on the spreadsheet or on a trading program. Then we either calculate the profits and losses manually or the program does it for us.

The most important aspect of a mechanical trading system is that it encompasses an automatic stop loss exit which is predetermined at the point of entry. This means that at the point of entry, the trader knows exactly what his or her maximum loss should be. All mechanical trading systems must be quantifiable and involve no human judgement.

Simple moving average trading rules

If we are using a simple moving average model, the instructions to be written are:

▦ **Enter buy long:** Close > Moving Average (Close, 20, Simple)
▦ **Exit long sell:** Close < Moving Average (Close, 20, Simple)
▦ **Enter sell short:** Close < Moving Average (Close, 20, Simple)
▦ **Exit short buy:** Close > Moving Average (Close, 20, Simple)

BBZ trading rules

If we are using the BBZ model, the instructions to be written are:

▦ **Enter buy long:** Close > BbandTop (Close, 20, Simple, 1)
▦ **Exit long sell:** Close < BbandTop (Close, 20, Simple, 1)
▦ **Enter sell short:** Close < BbandBot (Close, 20, Simple, 1)
▦ **Exit short buy:** Close > BbandBot (Close, 20, Simple, 1)

These can be created as a new system, which we call BBZ, in the trading program (see Figure 15.1).

Reading and analysing test results

Using the above simulation tests (which include transaction costs), the profit results for the FTSE 100 are shown in Table 15.1.

Table 15.1 BBZ profits for the FTSE 100: 2/1/2008–31/1/2008

Profit	603
Profitable to unprofitable trades	6 to 13
Average profit to average loss	274 to 80
Maximum consecutive losses	8 times totalling 635 points

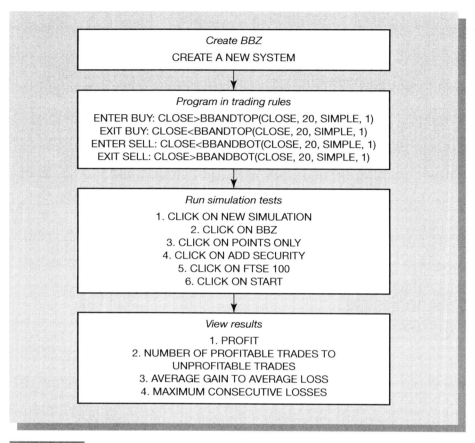

Figure 15.1   **Instructions on creating BBZ trading system**

Source: adapted from 'Appendix 1: Using Time Series Volatilities to Trade Trends' in *The Australian Technical Analysts Association Journal*, March/April 2005, p.37

As a comparison, a simple buy and hold is used. On 2/1/2008, the closing price was 6,416 and on 31/12/2008, the closing price was 4,434. A buy-and-hold policy in this case would have resulted in a loss of 2,023 index points. Using BBZ, the profit was a gain of 603 index points. Therefore, in this case, BBZ is better than a buy-and-hold policy.

However, the number of profitable trades, six, is too low compared to 13 unprofitable trades. The average profit of 274 index points is 3.4 times larger than the average loss of –80 index points, and makes up for the uneven number of profitable to unprofitable trades. The maximum consecutive losses of eight times, totalling 635 index points, is too high compared to the margin requirement of £4,105. A margin of £4,105 would allow the market to move 410.5 index points against the position.

Example

2008 profit using BBZ

Profit before transaction costs:

$$603 \times £10 = £6,030 \ (\$9,286) \text{ per FTSE 100 contract}$$

This is an annual return of 1.5 times the margin deposit of £4,105.

In this example, the eight consecutive losses of a total of 635 index points came after a big gain of 594 index points. Thus, the trader is able to take the losses financially and psychologically. A new trader who starts with these eight consecutive losses would have had repeated margin calls before making it to his or her next big gain of 846 index points. Trading requires a lot of patience and persistence.

This test profit can further be improved with optimisation. Optimisation aims to find the best value for the parameter, n (the number of periods), which is sensitive enough to catch the early part of a new trend and yet not generate too many false signals. A small percentage band may also be added on to the main technical indicator, so that only upon breaking beyond the band will the signal be acted upon. This band may be in percentage or absolute terms, which may be derived by eyeballing the relationship between the past price data and the selected technical indicator.

Chapter review

▪ A mechanical trading program is defined as a completely automated trading system. It can be in the form of software or it can be on a piece of paper. Having an objective mathematical trading program ensures that all trading decisions can be acted upon mechanically. All trades must be accounted for by the mechanical system when audited. Transparency is thus ensured.

▪ The trading rules on when to enter and exit can be written down in a trading program.

▪ A profit analysis table can be used for performance evaluation. A profit analysis checks for net profit, number of profitable trades to unprofitable trades, average profit to average loss and maximum consecutive losses to ensure that the trading capital is sufficient to last through bad times.

A NOTE TO THE TRADING APPRENTICE

The ideal trading system is not a perfect system

While it is the ambition of every trader to find the perfect trading system, as with any trading system there are always flaws, whether it is pattern recognition, Elliot wave counts or technical indicators like moving averages. So, the ideal trading system is not a perfect system but the one that makes the most return at the lowest risk and lowest number of false entries. It is every trader's quest to find the perfect trading system.

As too many trading systems are similar, it is best to design, construct and test a totally original trading system so that others will not know your support, resistance and especially your stop orders. This is to prevent your stops being triggered unnecessarily. Therefore, the ideal trading system is your own original, time-tested scheme.

Next we will specify the algorithm trading model that we use in the trading plan. The trading plan can be considered the blueprint for trading success because in it all the rules are clearly spelt out. A good trading plan shows a strategy to ensure the net outcome of trading is profitable.

16

How to write a good trading plan

What topics are covered in this chapter?

This chapter discusses:

- components of a good trading plan
- writing out the trading plan
- following the trading plan with discipline.

What are the objectives?

A trading plan is necessary because it is a map of successful trading strategies. Trading plans contain the trading rules that put the probability of winning in the long run in the trader's favour. To have a trading plan is to have a disciplined entry and exit without emotional constraints.

Trading is fun and exciting, but it does not fulfil the emotional or psychological need for winning, as in other games. Trading is a probability game, there is a 50% chance of winning and a 50% chance of losing. This is why you need to have a trading plan and strategies that give you a positive statistical profit edge.

Introduction

A trading plan is a blueprint of trading strategies that puts together all the technical knowledge that we have to put the probability of winning in our favour. A trading plan is what distinguishes winner traders from loser traders in the long term. Traders who win in the long run follow a trading plan with discipline while those who follow their emotions of greed and fear lose. All professional traders have trading plans.

Components of a good trading plan

A good trading plan specifies:

▦ the trading strategies

▦ the mathematical mechanical model to apply

▦ the amount to risk for the amount of expected reward

▦ the amount of capital required to start the trading business.

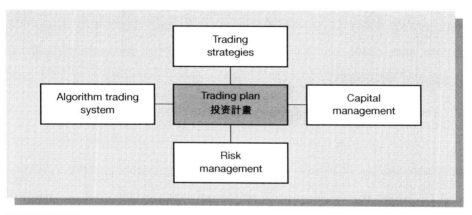

Figure 16.1   Components of a trading plan

You will learn all the components of a trading plan (see Figure 16.1). The trading plan is where you put your knowledge of technical tools and techniques together to make your trading business successful. It is a matter of identifying the trading strategy that puts the odds of winning in your favour.

The trading strategies

The strategies to use involve designing your own mechanical trading system that is well suited to the data series that you are familiar with. You have to design and build your own model because only then will you truly know how and why it works and have faith in it.

The trading strategy is to control your risk, preserve your capital and let your profit run. It begins with understanding the simplest probability theory in lay person's terms. The probability of any fair outcome is 50%: the probability of a winning trade is 50%. If the probability of winning and losing is the same, then the differentiating factor is the amount of winnings compared to the amount of losses. To emerge as a net winning trader, you need to keep the losses small (risk management) and the winnings large – as large as the market allows. Only then will you have net profit. This is your winning strategy. A trend trader who captures most of the trend and does not get whipsawed in range trading has the best proven strategy.

The market always works in your favour because it has a trending component. The trending component is your trading edge. Your trading strategy as a trend trader is to capture that trend as early as possible and your selected algorithm technical trading system will help you to do that.

Algorithm technical trading system

The mechanical mathematical trading system designed, built and selected is the one that makes the most profit, with the least consecutive losses and with at least equal chances of profitable and unprofitable trades.

The performance of the trading system can be backtested using the most current data. Then, the trader can choose the trading system that has at least equal chances of profitable and unprofitable trades. A high percentage of profitable trades will be good for the trader's psychology. However, the ultimate consideration is the trade with the highest return in monetary terms. Another consideration is that consecutive losses should not be so big that the trader's capital is unable to endure the accumulated losses.

BBZ is just a starting point and an example. You will want to design your own trading system along similar lines as you get more familiar with your own market.

Amount of risk for amount of reward to expect

The most important element in a trading plan is the maximum permissible loss per trade. This is the stop loss order placed at the same time as the entry order. At the point of entry, the trader knows exactly what his or her loss could be. He must be willing and prepared financially and mentally to part with this money. This is the exit requirement.

Therefore, the trading plan needs the trader to specify the expected reward to risk ratio. The purpose of this ratio is to determine if it is worth entering into the position. The larger the ratio, the more the risk is worth taking. The expected reward is gauged from the Fibonacci projection and previous high or low. The risk or stop loss, as a rule of thumb, is to be limited to one-third of the expected reward.

The minimum amount of capital required to start the trading business

Trading is a business, with profits and losses, risks and returns, and it requires sufficient capital. This is basically enough money to last through the first round of bad times (i.e. a series of consecutive losses).

Some people start a futures account during good times, meaning that their first few trades are profitable. From then on their futures trading businesses are set and they grow healthily. Some people start a futures account during bad times, meaning that the first few trades are unprofitable and their capital dwindles to an alarming low. If there is ever a margin call and they fail to top up the margin, that is the end of their trading business ventures. Some of them give up even before the margin call. However, those who last out the bad times are the ones who grow and shoot up in a trending market, after a series of whipsaws. The range market represents the bad times with losses as a series of whipsaws. After the range market, after the bands are so tight that they must burst, the market will definitely trend. It does not matter if the market is trending up or down. There is a huge profit to be made then, after the series of losses. Therefore, the minimum capital requirement must be enough funds to last through a series of losses in range trading.

Writing a trading plan

As in any business plan, you will need to put your plan in writing. Write down the trading rules for entry according to the specified algorithm technical trading model.

Some people – and they are right – consider exit trading rules to be most important. This is because you can control the loss but you should not control the gain. Therefore, contain the risk to one-third of potential profit. The projected profit is a function of the Fibonacci ratio, or the previous high or low.

It is a good idea to record every trade and the rationale behind it. You can treat this as a trading journal and use it for evaluation, eyeballing the trades and making fine adjustments.

BBZ is just a starting point and an example.

The entry trading rules are:

▨ Buy long when price > 1 standard deviation upper band.
▨ Sell short when price < –1 standard deviation lower band.

Entry considerations

Entry price:	5,136
Lower Bband:	5,184.8
Z-test:	−1.4
Fibonacci projection:	3,542
Previous low:	3,391.5 on 1/1/2003

Confirmed by

Volume:	Increasing volume from the previous day
Entry date/time:	23/9/2008 13:28
Projected profit:	1,594
Stop loss level:	**5,356 (220 index points)**
Reward/risk ratio:	1,594/220 = 7.2 times

Other reasons for entering the market

FTSE Eurofirst 300 is bursting out of the one standard deviation band on 22/9/2008. The mechanical trading rule signal is **sell short**

The automated signal and decision is to sell short because the close is lower than the lower band and the Z-test statistic is −1.4 (less than −1).

The projection level is 3,542. From the high of 6,730 on 8/10/2007 to the entry level of 5,136 is 1,594 index points. Another 1,594 index point fall will bring it to 3,542. This is assuming that 5,136 is the 50% Fibonacci ratio mark of the entire downtrend move beginning from 8/10/2007. The projection level is near the previous low of 3,391 on 1/1/2003.

The exit trading rule is the stop loss level, placed slightly higher than the previous day's high and also the moving average level. The stop loss is placed slightly higher to avoid any unnecessary whipsaws. Some scalpers like to trigger floods of stop loss orders at previous highs or the moving average level. (Scalpers are day traders who make a few points per trade in volume for a living.)

The stop loss point in this case is 220 index points, less than one-third of the projected profit. The reward to risk ratio is 7.2 times, more than the three times requirement, which makes the risk worth taking.

Note that the trade exit conditions need not be the same as the entry considerations. Professional traders usually have a more stringent exit requirement which tilts the winning odds in their favour. In risk management, the trailing stop can be a function of the previous day's range.

It is not enough just to have a written trading plan. More importantly, the trader needs to follow his or her own trading plan.

Following the trading plan with discipline

It is most unfortunate that a lot of people choose trading plans and then fail to follow them because they are overcome by their own feelings of greed and fear. With their greed they may try to outguess the trading system they have chosen to get earlier entries and try to make more profits. With their fear, they may want to hold on to losing positions and not cut losses, as the trading systems require, because they are afraid to lose.

Following the trading plan means not having to follow emotions, which are often detrimental to trading successfully. By following the trading plan, traders do not need to feel bad if they lose. This allows them to continue trading the plan until they make the big gain.

By following the trading plan, traders should not feel arrogant when they win. Arrogant people seldom make good traders because they follow themselves and not the market. By following trading plans with mechanical trading systems, our emotions are separated from our trading decisions.

Following a trading plan with discipline is essential to successful trading because of the probability of equal chances. However, this kind of winning is only applicable to traders who follow a trading plan that has a track record, with discipline. Without discipline, there is no need for a trading plan. Without a trading plan, the trader is anything but professional.

Trading is a game of probability. To win, the odds must be stacked in your favour. With a good trading plan and trading system, the odds have been shown to be in your favour. In order to calculate and control these odds, a linear trading program must be established. Linear trading means trading the same number of contracts.

Much discipline is required not to overtrade and to trade according to the plan. There is a tendency to increase the number of trading positions when the market is moving in your favour. This is called pyramiding. With pyramiding, the odds can no longer be controlled. If pyramiding works against you, it will be doubly hard to make back the profits that have been lost.

In backtesting, these extra losses have not been taken into account. Therefore, a linear trading program that is trading a constant number of contracts is always recommended.

Chapter review

▥ Winning traders follow a trading plan with discipline while losing traders follow their emotions of greed and fear. To have a trading plan is to have a disciplined entry and exit without emotional constraints. By following trading plans with mechanical trading systems, our emotions are separated from our trading decisions. Traders do not need to feel bad if they lose. This allows them to continue trading the plan until they make a big gain. In the same way, traders should not feel arrogant when they win. Arrogant people seldom make good traders.

▥ A trading plan is necessary because it specifies the amount to risk for the amount of reward to expect. The most important element in a trading plan is the maximum permissible loss. This is the stop loss order placed at the same time as the entry order.

▥ The algorithm technical trading system to use is the one that makes the most profit, with the least consecutive losses and with at least equal chances of profitable trades and losing trades.

A NOTE TO THE TRADING APPRENTICE

Trading plan

投资計畫

These Chinese characters mean investment plan. (The literal translation is 'cast money calculate draw'.)

Trading is a probability game. If we can calculate the probability and probable magnitude of winning, we can draw a detailed plan to encompass the possible outcomes of trading. If we can draw the binomial outcome tree with short losing branches and long winning branches, we can calculate the net probability of winning. This translates as the 50:50 rule that says if there are equal chances of winning and losing trades, the trading edge must lie in the larger magnitude of wins versus controlled losses.

▶

To a trader, it is very important to be able to draw the binomial probabilities of outcomes and calculate beforehand the net result of this business. Without a trading plan, the trader is lost, completely on his or her own, with primitive greed and fears. The trader has nothing to aim for, nothing to guide him or her and nothing to control losses. Most likely, he or she does not even have a mathematical mechanical model, like most amateur traders who enter the market on tips and rumours.

The trader must not reveal his or her trading plan to others, especially other traders. The trading plan must be private, especially the stop losses. This is because scalpers will try to make a living from triggering your stop losses. The trick is to place your stops where they will not be triggered unnecessarily.

The most important part of the trading plan is the money management and risk management components. Profiting from the trading plan is achieved by controlling the losses. All losses must be small. This is part of money management.

17

Losing a little to gain your capital

What topics are covered in this chapter?

You need enough capital to start the business of trading. The amount of capital required should be computable from the start of trading based on the professional technical trading system and the properties of the data series of the market you have chosen. Two of the ways to compute capital requirement are based on:

- maximum consecutive losses or
- winning versus losing percentages.

The final capital requirement should be the larger of these two.

What are the objectives?

The reason for having enough capital to sustain a series of small losses is to capture the big gain when the trend comes.

Introduction

Trading is about lasting through bad times. If your capital can last through the first series of bad times, it will definitely grow during the good times. The good times are the trending times. That is what I mean by built to last.

Maximum consecutive losses

One of first requirements of being a successful trader is to have enough capital to cover periods of maximum consecutive losses. We can use previous maximum consecutive losses as a guide to future losses. We only hope that future consecutive losses will not exceed the previous known maximum consecutive losses. We should be prepared for the worst case scenerio each time we enter the market, so that we do not give up before the big trend. The big trend usually comes after a period of frustrating small losses.

> **Example**
>
> If the maximum period of losses was eight trades with a maximum total of 635 index points from 28/7/2008 to 25/9/2008 then a 635 index point loss is equivalent to £6,350.
>
> Therefore, in this case, enough capital is the sum of the initial margin of £4,105 and the maximum consecutive losses of £6,350, totalling £10,455.

The maximum number of consecutive losses in the FTSE 100, for the period tested, is eight, amounting to £6,350. Psychologically, this will affect the emotional trader badly, but the professional trader will make it to the next big gain of 846 index points, £8,460. If the apprentice trader can make it to the big gain of 846, he or she is set to be a trader for life.

Winning versus losing percentages

Alternatively, enough capital can be calculated from the previous history of the trading model's percentage of gains versus losses. To calculate the percentage of the gains, take the gains of the trading model and divide this by the total gains and losses. Similarly, calculate the percentage of the losses against the total gains and losses.

> **Example**
>
> Gains: 1,648 → % gains   61%
>
> Losses: −1,045 → % losses 39%
>
> Initial margin: £4,105
>
> Enough capital   100/(61 − 39) × £4,105 = £18,659.

Use the higher of the two values as the minimum capital. Remember transaction costs should be factored in as well. Therefore, in this example, £18,659 is deemed sufficient for use in the next quarter. The equity curve of the amount of capital in the account for 2008 looks like that shown in Figure 17.1.

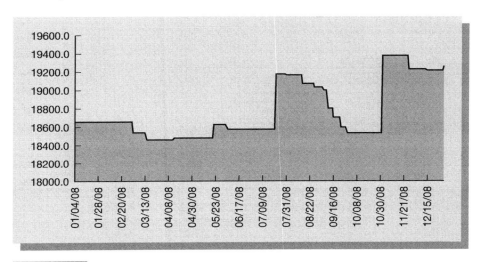

Figure 17.1   BBZ equity curve for the FTSE 100: year 2008

Chapter review

▓ One of first requirements of being a successful trader is to have enough capital to cover periods of maximum consecutive losses.

▓ Capital requirement calculations can also be based on the winning–losing percentage of the chosen proprietary trading system based on previous data of the chosen market.

▓ To be conservative, the professional trader is advised to take the larger of the two calculations.

A NOTE TO THE TRADING APPRENTICE

Do not gamble with your life savings – manage your capital well

If you have spent your whole life saving, it does not make sense to gamble it away with one trade. Manage your life savings well by limiting your losses to what you can afford to lose each time until you make the big gain from the impending trend. If, in backtesting, the maximum consecutive loss is eight times, then limit your losses to one-eighth of your capital minus the margin. The rule is never lose your margin.

However, some professional traders would recommend that you do not lose more than one-third of your capital at any one time. I would agree with this for your general investment portfolio, especially if you keep half of your portfolio investment in bonds and money market instruments. However, for your futures account, because of the higher risk and return factor as well as the leverage factor, be careful not to lose more than half your capital.

Money management is in fact risk management with adequate capital. The important thing to remember about trading is that it is not luck when you win or lose: it is risk management and the disciplined act of cutting losses.

The trick here is to have enough capital to handle the maximum consecutive losses before the big break comes. Professional traders do not consider this as a trick but a capital requirement for their trading business. Having enough capital for trading is equivalent to having enough cash flow to sustain a business.

In fact, trading is a series of cutting losses. It need not be painful if you trade with discipline. An automated stop loss order is the easiest way to exit the market.

18

Practise stop loss

What are the objectives?

- After learning and practising the 'cut loss early' habit with discipline, new traders are well on their way to becoming professional traders. The disciplined act of cutting losses early is the qualifying mark of becoming a professional trader because profit amounts will exceed the small losses in big trend movements. In summary, trading is all about cutting losses early, so the losses are small.

- It is necessary to control and keep losses small enough for when a big profit finally comes. When the big trend profit comes, it should exceed the total amount of the small losses. Only then will your net trading experience be positive.

What topics are covered in this chapter?

Putting your good-till-cancel (GTC) stop loss order at the point of entry is the most disciplined and easiest way of cutting your loss. Only if the market moves in the direction of your trade should you follow with a trailing stop. This chapter will discuss:

- automatic GTC stop loss at order at point of entry

- trailing stops.

Introduction

Risk management in trading is synonymous with the disciplined action of cutting losses early. Cutting losses is the first and the hardest lesson that professional traders learn and master. This is because losses should always be controlled.

Losing is part of the game. The people who do not want to lose small will almost certainly ultimately lose big. If they do not cut their losses early and the market never reverses to let them out at profit or at cost, this will ultimately result in huge losses for them.

Automatic GTC stop loss order at point of entry

Risk management is all about cutting loss. Expect to lose and predict the amount of loss. Your trading plan should factor this in.

In the BBZ system, like most trading systems, at the point of entry there is a 50% chance that the trade will be a loss. Therefore, you should expect that loss and control it by using an automatic good-till-cancel (GTC) stop loss order.

Traders must place their automatic GTC stop loss orders at the point of entry. Their stop loss may be at such significant levels as the previous high/low or resistance/support. Some of the professional trading models use stop loss levels that are functions of the previous day's range.

In this way, traders can calculate their losses, which must be controlled and kept low. At the point of entry, professional traders are able to calculate the maximum losses if markets go against their trading signals. There is no such thing as unexpected losses as reported in the press.

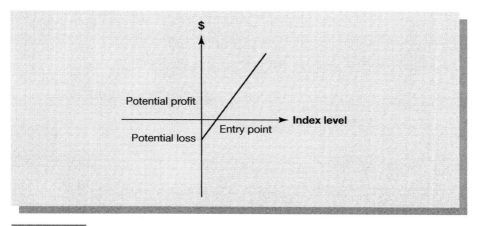

Figure 18.1   Profit and loss chart for a long position with stop loss order

If you are long a futures contract, your potential loss is limited to your stop loss level, but with a trailing stop loss order, as the market rises (a rising index level) your profit continues to grow. Your potential loss–profit line looks like that in Figure 18.1.

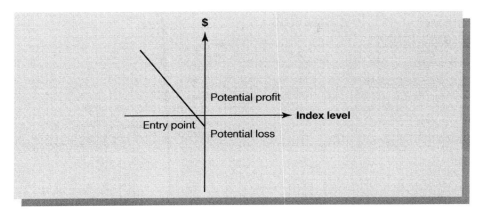

Figure 18.2   **Profit and loss chart for a short position with stop loss order**

If you are short a futures contract, your potential loss is limited to your stop loss level, but with a trailing stop loss order, as the market falls (a falling index level), your profit continues to grow. Your potential loss–profit line looks like that in Figure 18.2.

Example

BBZ

23/9/2008

Sell short signal	5,136
Stop loss level	5,356
Expected loss	220 index points

Trailing stops

If the stop you place is not triggered, the market is moving in the direction of your position. You may then revise your stop in the market's direction: this is called a trailing stop. This may be a boring mechanical way to trade but it is the most stress-free way known for repeatedly healthy profit performance.

BBZ

24/9/2008

Price	5,095.0
Lower band	5,185
Previous GTC stop loss	5,356

Revise stop from 5,356 to 5,185.

Note that different traders have different risk tolerance levels. The stop should be placed where it will not be triggered unnecessarily.

Chapter review

▪ Losses should always be controlled. Cutting losses is the first and hardest lesson that professional traders learn and master. You must control and keep the losses small enough for the profits, when they come, to exceed the total amount of the small losses.

▪ Professional traders place their automatic GTC stop loss orders at the point of entry. In this way, they can calculate the exact loss they are exposed to.

▪ If the market moves in their direction, they revise their stops in a trailing manner.

A NOTE TO THE TRADING APPRENTICE

The first cut may be painful but the last cut kills

Psychological counselling may be required in dealing with the loss the trader him or herself cuts but if the trading house ever has to cut the loss for a trader then he or she is beyond financial repair.

Therefore, the first and most important lesson in trading is how to cut a loss early. Not until the new apprentice can learn how to take small losses and carry on trading is he or she truly qualified as a professional trader. To do so is to follow the cut loss trading plan, which is to place the stop loss order at the point of entry.

It is my observation that people rarely know how to cut losses themselves, so it is best when the trading system automatically does it for them. This is done by keying in a GTC stop loss order at the onset of a new trading position.

19

Fine tuning the trading wheels

What topics are covered in this chapter?

A simple trading journal sheet is prepared for evaluation purposes. The important items are actual losses versus permissible losses and actual gains versus realised gains. This chapter discusses:

- periodic post-mortem evaluation of trades
- comparison of realised and unrealised losses and gains.

What are the objectives?

The purpose of the trade evaluation is:

- to trace common patterns in the trades
- to evaluate the actual realised return against the projected profit and the actual realised losses against the permissible risk.

If followed with discipline, the actual realised losses should be the stop loss levels or the permissible risk.

Introduction

The final step is to record every trade and then evaluate them periodically for ways to avoid unnecessary losing trades and to improve the timing of the winning trades. Unfortunately, this is the step most unprofessional traders are too lazy to do. Fortunately, this step is actually easy to carry out, especially with a pre-prepared trading journal sheet.

Periodic post-mortem evaluation of trades

Although a periodic post-mortem evaluation of trades may be conducted at regular intervals, the trade evaluation journal should be ready for any ad-hoc inspection. It would be ideal if the periodic evaluation could be conducted at the mid-cycle of each phase. This will assess the parameters that are most fitting to the current phase. However, it is difficult, if not impossible, to guesstimate the middle point of the range or trend. Thus, it is recommended that an ad-hoc evaluation and optimisation is conducted between periodic evaluations. Compare the ad-hoc evaluation against the periodic evaluation and adjust the parameters, if necessary, accordingly.

In an institutional proprietary trading desk, trade evaluation is done jointly by the chief dealer and the trading system designer. They can run optimisation tests for more fitting parameters and can also eyeball the spreadsheets of the trade evaluation journal.

Trade evaluations are done to trace a common pattern in the losing trades and to check if there is a way to get earlier confirmation for the winning trades. Slight adjustments that quicken or lessen the sensitivity of the mechanical trading systems may be made. The objective is the same, to make the least losses with maximum profits. Below is a very simple example of a blank trade evaluation sheet, specifying the minimum requirements for entry and exit considerations.

TRADE EVALUATION JOURNAL

Entry considerations	*Exit considerations*
Entry price: _____	Exit price: _____
Bband: _____	Bband: _____
Z-test: _____	Z-test: _____
Fibonacci projection: _____	*Confirmed by*
Previous high/low: _____	Volume _____
Confirmed by	Exit date/time _____
Volume: _____	Actual gain/loss _____
Entry date/time: _____	Reward/risk ratio _____
Projected profit: _____	*Reasons for gains/losses*
Stop loss level: _____	Trading system _____
Reward/risk ratio: _____	Trader execution _____
Other reasons for entering the market: _____	Other comments_____
Trading decision: short/long	_____

Comparisons of realised and unrealised losses and gains

Actual loss versus permissible loss

The actual loss on the day of initiation of the trade will be the stop loss level plus one or a few ticks slippage. If the market moves in the direction of your trade, the actual loss will be where you adjusted your trailing stop order to. Therefore, the actual loss should be the initial stop loss level or less.

TRADE EVALUATION JOURNAL

Short entry considerations

Entry price: 5,136

Lower Bband: 5,184.8

Z-test: −1.4

Fibonacci projection: 3,542

Previous low: 3,391.5 on 1/1/2003

Confirmed by

Volume: Increasing volume from the previous day

Entry date/time: 23/9/2008 13:28

Projected profit: 1,594

Stop loss level: 5,356 (220 index points)

Reward/risk ratio: 1,594/220 = 7.2 times

Other reasons for entering the market: FTSE Eurofirst 300 is bursting out of the one standard deviation band on 22/9/2008

Trading Decision: Short

Bought back exit considerations

Exit price: 5,185.5

Lower Bband: 5,175

Z-test: −0.9

Confirmed by

Volume: Increasing volume from the previous day

Exit date/time: 25/9/2008 13:00

Actual loss: −49.5 index points

Actual loss/permissible loss: −49.5/220 = −0.225

Reasons for smaller loss:

Trading system: Trailing stop

Trader Execution: 0.5 index point slippage

Other comments: Transaction costs of 1 index point. The trend is still down. This exit could have been avoided if a longer period was used: 37 days is used for BBZ.

Because of the trailing stop revision we made on 24/9/2008 from 5,356 to 5,185, the actual loss is smaller than was budgeted for. As long as the market starts to move in the direction of the trade, the loss will be adjusted to be smaller.

Another evaluation angle is to fine tune by using a longer period moving average and standard deviation such as 37 days. This would have prevented the position shown above from being triggered unnecessarily because in hindsight we can see it is the beginning of a major downtrend.

Actual profit versus projected profit

In accordance with the trading system, always exit on the stop order when the market reverses. Even if the market hits your initial target price, let the profit run. This is the simplest way to make a profit. It is common for the apprentice trader to want to exit at the target price using a limit order. Experienced traders know that when the market trends, it often gives extra bonus points, much more than expected. So, do not guesstimate the market: let it tell you what to do.

Of course, the other case is when your target price is too far away and is never reached. In this case, you will similarly exit after the market reverses, at the signal to do so. Your actual profit is less than your projected profit and you may have been too optimistic.

Example

Trade evaluation journal

Short entry considerations	*Bought back exit considerations*
Entry price: 5,088.5	Exit price: 4,242.5
Lower Bband: 5,184.8	Lower Bband: 4,090.3
Z-test: –1.4	Z-test: –0.7
Fibonacci projection: 3,542	*Confirmed by*
Previous low: 3,391.5 on 1/1/2003	Volume: Increasing volume from the previous day
Entry date/time: 26/9/2008 13:01	
Projected profit: 1,546.5	Exit date/time: 29/10/2008 13:12
Stop loss level: 5,158 **(69.5 index points)**	Actual gain: 846 index points
	Actual gain/Projected gain: 846/1,546.5 = 0.55
Reward/risk ratio: 1,546.5/69.5 = 22.2 times	*Reasons for smaller gain*:
Other reasons for entering the market:	Overestimation of projected profit.
FTSE Eurofirst 300 is bursting out of the one standard deviation band on 22/9/2008	*Other comments*: Transaction costs of 1 index point
Trading decision: Short	

In some academic studies, the trading results are tested for significance. The purpose of doing this is to prove that a mechanical trading system generates a profit above that of a buy-and-hold strategy. In any case, it is wise to look back on past mistakes in order to perform better in the future.

Chapter review

▦ The final step in trading is to record each and every trade and then carefully evaluate what went right and what went wrong.

▦ The purpose of the trade evaluation is to assess the actual realised return against the projected return and the actual realised losses against the permissible risk. If followed with discipline, the actual realised losses should be the stop loss levels or the permissible risk.

▦ A periodical post-mortem of trade evaluation sheets should be undertaken to trace a common pattern in the losing trades and to check if there is a way to get earlier confirmation for the winning trades. Slight adjustments that quicken or lessen the sensitivity of the mechanical trading systems may be made.

A NOTE TO THE TRADING APPRENTICE

Post-mortem of trades is not only the job of the chief dealer

It is best to do an evaluation objectively as if you were the chief dealer. First, check and compare the differences between expected results and actual results. Make no excuse for indiscipline, whether it results in losses or gains. Second, check and eyeball to see if you can achieve better results by changing the parameters of your trading model to suit current market conditions.

However, do not be too harsh on yourself. Refine your trading model if need be and put past mistakes to the back of your mind. Start afresh with your model.

Even if the whole proprietary trading model set-up had been carefully laid out for you for immediate execution and all the necessary steps had been prepared for you to start trading professionally, the actual trading results would differ from individual to individual due to the trading attitudes that they adopt.

20

The total trader – winning trading psychology

What topics are covered in this chapter?

How do we differentiate a trading winner from a loser? The 10 typical characteristics to look out for are:

- the overconfident tips and rumours monger
- the person in the crowd
- the fortune teller
- Mr/Ms Always Right
- Mr/Ms Perseverance
- Mr/Ms Ultra Rich who does not care about losses
- the person who refuses to place stop loss orders at the initiation of a new position
- the person who does not believe in his or her own trading system
- the stubborn technician who refuses to change with time no matter how many losses he or she has made
- the behaviourial scientist.

What are the objectives?

It is important to remember that professional traders do not make profits all the time: they do not make losses all the time either. When they make losses, they make sure the losses are small. When they make profits, they let the profits run. In this way, the net result of their trading will be gain.

Introduction

The final element that distinguishes long-term winners from losers is trading attitude.

Those who never want to cut losses will be the losers when forced to do so as all their margins are depleted. They, of course, do not follow any trading plan or system because all trading plans or systems have cut loss stops at the entry point.

Long-term winners follow trading systems and cut losses whenever the stop loss prices are triggered. Long-term winners also never give up after a series of small losses because they believe in their chosen trading systems and they do not change them before the big gain. The periods of a series of small losses in range trading are usually periods of accumulation or distribution by large market players.

Trading psychological test

Conditions before entering or exiting a position

1.	Check with other traders for their views of the market.	Yes/No
2.	Ask others about their positions and tell them about yours.	Yes/No
3.	Buy at an all-time low and sell at an all-time high, all the time.	Yes/No
4.	Enter and exit the position at target price.	Yes/No
5.	Have perseverance to hold on to a long-term position.	Yes/No
6.	Have large capital to hold on to one position through the bad times.	Yes/No
7.	Try to win all the time.	Yes/No
8.	See profit, take it immediately.	Yes/No
9.	If there are a few losses, stop trading immediately.	Yes/No
10.	Must have a good feel for the market.	Yes/No

Total mark

▓ Give yourself –1 mark for a Yes and +1 for a No.

▓ Tally the marks together and read the results below.

If you receive a 6 and above, you are well on your way to becoming a wonderful trader: congratulations. If you receive 0 to 5, you are on your way to becoming a professional trader but there is still some hard work to do or some habits to discard. If you receive anything less than 0, do read the book again before you commit to your first trade.

Trading is a lone game. You do not always need to talk or check with others, regarding their views and their positions. They are not always right, especially the tipsters and rumour mongers. In my experience, the first time I hear that a stock is going to run up is usually right, the second time is sometimes correct but the third time is usually wrong. The rationale for this is that after a period of accumulation (near the lows), the stockists will give out rumours that they are going to push the stocks to their friends. This accounts for the first wave of buying. The second wave of buying begins for those who missed the first boat, when the price retraces a little. By the end of this impulsive uptrend wave, the stockists are giving out bullish facts on the stocks while they sell to the greedy public. So, stay away from rumour mongers and stockists. Your chart can and will tell you when to buy when the stock bursts up from its trading range after the accumulation period. Your chart will also indicate when to sell, probably after the stockists finish selling.

If you can buy at the very lowest point and sell at the very highest point all the time, you do not have to read this book. Most of us usually buy near the low and sell near the high, when our technical indicators tell us to.

The biggest technical lie is put about by those who set enter target and then exit target according to certain counts/observations. Usually, they will gain many small profits and a few large losses. It will be good if their small profits cover the large losses. However, generally the small profits cannot cover their numerous transaction costs.

The other technical lie is put about by those who subscribe to a buy-and-hold policy for a futures contract. When their positions are against them, they say that these are long-term investments. I have seen many of them lose all their capital in futures by subscribing to this policy. They are the big stockists in the stock market who take little profits when they see them but refuse to cut losses when the positions are against them. They must be the ones who are right in the stock market and in stock picking. They tell people that they always make money in the market, which is only half the truth. The other half, which they keep quiet, is that their positions are automatically cut at large losses at the end of the month when the current month futures contract expires against them. They are the ones who do not put small stop loss orders at the initiation of their positions and do not have the willpower to cut their losses manually.

Finally, after a few imposed cut losses, they quit the futures market to concentrate again on small stock gains on big volume. Their accounts are dangerous because they represent unlimited risk with no workable trading strategy.

Professional traders have trend trading systems. However, there are times when the traders just change trading techniques from trending to ranging only to lose again because the market finally trends. Therefore, I suggest traders should take a long-term view of the probabilities that the next move is going to be a trending move after a series of small range trading moves. The probabilities can be guesstimated from previous historical price performance. If the worst case scenario is eight consecutive losses in a row over the past 10 years, the chance of a ninth consecutive loss in a row is very slim.

Finally, I do not know what to say about the behavioural scientists who want to explain everything about why the market, the people in the market or the herd mentality behave in the way that they do. I only say it is enough to profit from our technical indicators to buy when the herd mentality decides to push the market up in a buying frenzy and sell when the crowd sells in a panic selling. The herd mentality accounts for our big uptrend and downtrend waves.

Chapter review

■ Those who never want to cut a loss will be the losers when they are forced to do so when all their margins are depleted.

■ They, of course, do not follow any trading plan or system because all trading plans or systems have cut loss stops at the entry point.

■ Long-term winners follow trading systems and cut losses whenever the stop loss prices are triggered. Long-term winners also never give up after a series of small losses because they believe in their chosen trading systems and they do not change them before the big gain.

A NOTE TO THE TRADING APPRENTICE

What has behaviourial finance got to do with quantitative trading?

Herd mentality, overconfidence, biased judgements and loss aversion are said to be behaviourial factors affecting the markets. What have these got to do with quantitative trading? I don't know the answer. My observation from experience dealing with investors finds that:

▨ overconfidence has led to biased judgements

▨ loss aversion has led to bigger losses.

As it is pointless to argue about the rationality behind these market participants' behaviours, it is much more realistic and profitable to look at the hard statistics of the market's behaviour itself and the past performance of algorithm trading systems, and then find the suitable money making algorithm trading system for a lucrative market. Don't you agree that we could be quietly making money ourselves with our trading systems rather than engaging in futile efforts that argue for technical analysis and behavioural finance?

Do you realise now that we don't need to know and explain why the market does what it does? It is more important just to follow your proven trading system mechanically. Let the others explain the market if they want to. Let us not get distracted from trading objectively and quantitatively with our time tested algorithm trading system.

Whatever the behaviour of market participants we are still concerned with the same subjects: attitudes to risk management and money management. If the young trading apprentice can manage risk exposure and thus money at risk, he or she will be well on the way to becoming a professional trader.

Conclusion: the complete trading set-up kit

What topics are covered in this conclusion?

- What can go wrong?
- Is trading futures for you?

What are the objectives?

The primary objective of this book is to start you trading in the professional way with an expectation of a net positive statistical return. The specific objectives are to first equip you with technical analysis knowledge, as the world knows it, then select and innovate appropriate technical indicators to make your own trading system. The ultimate objective is for you to be a professional trader who makes a profit in the long run.

Introduction

The most important conclusion that we are able to draw from all that we have learnt is never to trade without a model. All professional traders have their own trading models. In this book, we have laid out the 10 steps to building a very basic and simple professional trading model from scratch.

The process involves data analysis in order to choose the right tools, techniques, formulas and software. The most important element of a trading plan is the risk management aspect which emphasises how to control losses. Without a stop loss order at the point of entry, there is no way to guesstimate the chances of winning against losing. Capital must be sufficient to cover periods of consecutive losses.

The final step to trading is to evaluate what went right, what went wrong and how the model can be improved further. Any system improvement or fine tuning must be done at regular intervals, far enough apart for the results (profits) to be reaped. A system improvement may also be done after a large gain following a period of small consecutive losses.

Overall, the trading attitude is the most important human element that distinguishes winners from losers. Winners are strong enough to know that the chances of losing are 50% and to cut their losses when the losses are small. They never leave losses to enlarge. They know that they are playing a game of probability and the only way to win is to keep their losses small. Then, the odds of them winning where there are big trends are huge.

What can go wrong?

Model trading is simple and without real-life emotions. Trading in reality is much more dangerous than paper model trading. Professional traders agree that they can define and control the dangers. The known dangers are slippage, not getting filled at the triggered price but at some price worse than the stop loss price, and prices whipsawing (which we did not capture using end-of-day closing prices).

The results from backtesting models are different from the actual profits from live trading (recorded over the same period). The differences are:

▦ slippage (we may not get the price we want because of thin market conditions)

▦ intraday whipsaws (the market may give false signals, i.e. touch the trigger price and move back to where it came from)

▦ extra rollover transaction costs (the signal is still on, the month is expiring and we need to roll over to the next month)

▦ rollover points

▦ earlier entry and exit.

While slippage, intraday whipsaws and extra rollover transaction costs result in less profit than that from backtesting, the rollover points from a current month to the next may sometimes be extra gains not recorded in the backtesting. Backtesting uses the closing prices while in live trading we enter the positions immediately when we get the signals. This will result in more gains than those reported from backtesting.

The final conclusion is that technical analysis is a science not an art. There may be some subjective art to the trading techniques that a privileged few seem to have but we cannot scientifically prove this. However, we can scientifically and objectively prove that the BBZ mechanical trading system based on technical analysis concepts of moving average and standard deviations could make us a profit consistently in the long term.

Is trading futures for you?

Trading futures for a living takes years of research, besides incurring many trading losses, to find a trading model that you can bet your money on.

Futures involve high leverage as they are traded on small margins. Therefore, both the risk exposure and loss potential is huge, but returns can be very high. As in finance theory, for the high amount of risk exposure, you expect substantial rewards.

Trading futures involves managing and controlling the risks and losses via good money management. Good money management entails having enough cash flow to trade a big trend after a series of small losses. If you can manage that, you have passed the first qualifying mark of being a professional trader.

If you are considering becoming a futures broker representative, you need to assess many factors like business viability, your network of contacts and the potential business they can bring besides your own financial ability to withstand periods when the market is ranging. In these periods, unless you are the accumulation or distribution agent for the large players, volume and trading opportunities are low. If you can withstand such tough conditions, you have the makings of becoming a futures broker representative.

Conclusion review

This book attempts to conduct a quick, simple trading apprenticeship programme in 10 steps. It is a trading methodology that you can adopt as a trading habit. By reading this book, you have taken a short cut through years of losses and research to become a professional trader.

Before you even think of beginning to trade, the first step is to do your own research on the price series. The second step is to choose your preferred tools and your particular style of using them (which may not be the same as the way others use them). All trading models must be mechanical and followed with discipline. If you pick and choose the signals that coincide with fundamental research reports generated by broking houses, they are almost always the wrong signals – ones that result in losses. The trading plan is what separates the professional trader from the amateur. A trading plan must include a risk management mechanism – also called a cut loss early programme. Because markets trend, as long as there are cut loss strategies at the point of entry, the net result of any disciplined trading can only be profit. Trade evaluation is the post mortem conducted to find common patterns on the losing streak and make adjustments to improve trading. Finally, it is traders' attitudes that make them professionals or gamblers. The ones who follow the rules are the professionals. Gamblers make big profits and bigger losses – they are ruled by greed.

A NOTE TO THE TRADING APPRENTICE

The exceptional trader is not a superstar trader

The exceptional trader is not:

▨ the busiest trader who overtrades and thus overloses

▨ the busybody trader who knows and trades every rumour and tip in the market

▨ the flashiest trader in town with the flashiest car, sunglasses and smile posing for any reporter who is looking for an article to write.

In the short run, such traders may be making huge profits but you never hear of them again after they make the equally huge losses. In fact, you never knew some of them until they made the huge losses. I don't think it is your goal to be a superstar trader. Dreams of being one are for the young and naïve. If you are realistic, choose to be a professional trader.

Remember, as a professional, you must do your own research before you trade in any market. The very least you need for data analysis are the relevant statistics: the averages and the standard deviations for prices and volume. The most basic trading system, based on moving average, is the standard test. Some academic studies have shown that as markets get more sophisticated, the common moving average trading systems are not as lucrative as they used to be. So test how accurate the signals are in bull markets and in bear markets. This will determine if your trading model is suitable to the market in which you want to trade.

You must write out a trading plan that specifies the mechanical trading model that you have chosen. The mechanical model must be backtested using previous data. One of the most important requirements is to test for maximum consecutive losses, so that you have sufficient capital to last before the big trend sets in.

Remember to do regular trade evaluations at periodic intervals. This is so that you can make adjustments to avoid unnecessary wrong trades and perform system optimisations so that you can get into a trend as early as possible. In reviewing past trades, write down any particular comments about the market such as duration of the accumulation or distribution period. A trading spreadsheet may be set up to include price and volume analysis, stage analysis, a standard 20-day moving average test, trend analysis, standard deviation analysis, model backtesting, signal accuracy and optimisation.

Therefore, the exceptional trader is:

▨ the professional trader who has done his or her own research on his or her selected markets

▨ the mentally prepared trader who is willing to accept small losses for huge gains

■ the serious trader who is quietly making money in the market with his or her own proprietary statistically proven trading system while others are making noise about fundamental reports, headlines and random walk arguments.

You have got what it takes to be an exceptional trader – the positive statistical edge of abnormal returns. You have got a unique technical trading tool that is your very own, innovated specially for your market to help you make the abnormal returns you can expect. As an exceptional trader, there is no room or need for luck. Trading is a serious business but it is also fun. Have fun with your fund – let it grow and build it to last. Finally, I say let it grow, not make it grow, because with a proven technical trading system the abnormal returns come automatically.

Getting started

Trading is the most exciting profession in the world for me and I hope it is for you too. It is a serious profession because it involves people's life savings. I know you are serious about trading because you took the time to read this book to the end. There is only one way to get started – chart your own trading. You have all the tools to start. Use the tools in this book and then develop your own unique trading system. Many others have done it and so can you.

You now have the extra proven statistical edge to ensure that your capital grows at an abnormal return rate in the long run. Use it. Use the knowledge you have gained in this book to first research the markets and then design your own trading model. Your trading model may not be perfect. The idea is to keep improving it to make maximum profits at any given time.

I hope that the technical analysis concepts work for you as they do for many others. You are now on a level with other professional traders. The next step is to exceed this level: that is, to develop your own unique trading model for your market.

Always remember the 10 trading rules that I keep repeating – they are important so here they are again in summary.

THE 10 MOST IMPORTANT TRADING RULES

1 Do your own research

This task is too important to leave to the research analysts. You have to read your own charts and no one else can do this for you. Markets change all the time and your parameters need to be adjusted according to these changes. So change them and keep quiet about it.

2 Whatever others tell you regarding the market is noise: believe only your mechanical trading system

Do not talk to others about your position. Do not ask others for their market opinions. Never listen to anyone who wants to tell you about the market. If they really knew, they would not be talking about it. Professional traders call this cheap market talk 'noise'. You have all you need to get going – your powerful mechanical trading system that automatically generates trading signals. Follow it, especially the stop loss. With a mechanical trading system, there is no need to guesstimate and there is no need to fear. Granted, it takes a lot of hard work to develop your trading system. You have to do the hard work because your mechanical trading system is your statistical edge of net positive return.

3 Don't get greedy – do only linear trading

To keep loss control simple, only do linear trading: that is, trade the same number of contracts all the time. Do not increase the number of contracts as you start to profit. Your last trades may be losing ones. Do not decrease the number of contracts as you lose to meet margin requirements because you may not make back the loss you have donated to the market. The easiest, simplest and most objective money management strategy is to do linear trading. However, as you become more experienced, you may consider writing a formula for objectively and mechanically increasing the number of contracts after each range trading whipsaw loss.

4 Do not be satisfied with small profits. Follow your trading model. We are talking about trend trading

If the market is trending, hold on to the position and profit by trailing stops. I have argued many times for new traders to hang on to winning positions and not take small profits. Small profits and small losses equals losses in transaction costs. There is only one equation for trend trading, large gains and small losses, which not only cover transaction costs but also your precious time spent trading.

5 Put in your GTC stop order at entry point

Trading is all about controlling loss. You will lose some of the time, so cut your loss early. In fact, expect to lose 50% of the time. Be disciplined. Put in a GTC cut loss order at entry point.

6 Do not panic or fear, your stops are here

There is never any need to panic or fear because your stops will take care of your positions. That is why you must have stops at the moment of entry. You should prepare for the worst, which is your stop loss point.

7 Be disciplined! Your trailing stops are the only way to liquidate a position. Never give limit or market orders to your broker to get out

Adjust your trailing stops as often as the market moves in your direction. Never stop believing your trading system – never get out too early.

8 Always have enough capital to last through bad times

You must have enough capital to sustain you over a period of maximum consecutive losses. This will enable you to hang in there until the big trend sets in.

9 Forget all past losses: start anew

Evaluate your own performance on a regular basis and then forget all about past losses and mistakes. Agonising over past losses will not make you a professional trader.

10 Be professional at all times!

Be professional about your losses especially. If you lose a few times in a row, it is not the end of the world as long as you have enough capital to sustain you to the next big trend.

These are the simplest and most common trading rules that all professional traders know and practise. If you can follow these rules with discipline, you will graduate to be a professional trader when the big trend runs set in. Test these 10 simple steps and put their principles to work to make money for you in the long run.

What's next?

Algorithm trading draws its automated trading decisions from a variety of factors including technical analysis signal generations and analysis of time series statistics and artificial intelligence. The next step in quantitative trading is to combine the technical analysis concepts and indicators that you learnt here with conventional time series methods like AR-GARCH, genetic algorithm programing, or neural networks and other adaptive methods to produce superior models that generate abnormal returns in excess of the buy-and-hold policy.

This is the recommendation for future research. This new field of trading continues to generate such growing interest compared to the unquantifiable trading decision making of the older generation of speculators, that new supporting functions such as model validator and hardware modifier for statistical arbitrage are emerging. It can be concluded that in search of abnormal returns, many new studies in artificial intelligence, genetic programing and combinations of methods are emerging to overshadow old theories like the passive random walk theory that advocates the do-nothing strategy.

Additional notes

The next step is to try to find an adaptive technical indicator that can discriminate between range trading and trend trading. Instead of expecting the market to adapt to the preset technical indicators, your algorithm trading system should be flexible enough to adjust its parameters immediately to the different types of market conditions; range market or trend market. An example of one simple approach is to build in an adjusting mechanism. Gandolfi *et al.* (2008) suggest a dynamic volatility indicator: the ratio of the 10-day standard deviation of closing prices divided by the 50-day average of the standard deviation of closing prices. The adjustable Bands Z-Test-Statistics (ABZ) algorithm trading system uses a long-term 34-day standard deviation of closing prices divided by a short-term six-day standard deviation of closing prices. This new technical indicator is called the efficacy ratio. Using the same concept as BBZ, ABZ trades only outside the 0.8 standard deviation bands.

If the long-term prices are less volatile than short-term prices, we use a shorter moving average and narrower standard deviation bands. When current prices are more volatile, this allows a faster entry into the new trend. If the long-term prices are more volatile than short-term prices, we use a longer moving average and wider standard deviation bands. When current prices are less volatile, this helps to avoid some whipsaws in a range market. The efficacy ratio adjusts the moving average length and standard deviation automatically.

On preliminary testings, ABZ shows a profit of 949 index points for the FTSE 100, 42 index points for Korea's KOSPI, 27.6 index points for Singapore's SiMSCI and 316 index points for Malaysia's FKLI for the year 2008. It also shows a profit of 22 for Soybean Futures and 690 for FCPO (Malaysia's Futures on Crude Palm Oil) for 2008.

However, there is much room for future research, testing and work to define the short-term and long-term standard deviation before the model can be accepted and validated, which could take years. Welcome to the club and join the search for the 'perfect' trading system.

All the best in your trading career.

Glossary

Absolute range breakout system An n number of days breakout system is to buy on breakup above the last n days trading range and to sell on breakdown below the last n days trading range.

Algorithm trading system A trading system with pre-set trading rules to mathematically compute, according to an algorithm (suitable to the prevailing market conditions), mechanically generated signals on when to enter and when to exit the market. The algorithm is derived after intensive backtesting and optimisation. Algorithm trading is employed by the professional model trading desks of large financial institutions.

Ask The price that a seller is willing to receive for a contract.

Average directional index (ADX) A leading indicator to evaluate the strength of the current trend. ADX is derived from +DI and –DI. A buy signal occurs when +DI > –DI. A sell signal occurs when –DI > +DI. If ADX > 40, the trend is strong. If ADX < 20, the trend is weak. If ADX is changing from below 20 to above 20, the market is said to be changing from a range trading mode to a trend trading mode.

Bands Lines constructed around a moving average that define, in relative terms, what is high and what is low.

Bar chart A type of chart with vertical bars representing trading. The top of each bar is the period's high and the bottom of the bar is the period's low. The tick to the left is the opening price and the tick to the right is the closing price.

Bearish market A market in which prices are expected to be declining.

Bid The price that a buyer is willing to pay for a contract.

Bollinger bands A type of band that is constructed as a default two standard deviations around a default 20-day moving average. Often abbreviated to Bbands. John Bollinger is the originator of Bollinger Bands. More information can be found in his book, *Bollinger on Bollinger* (2002)

Bottoms and tops A double/triple bottom is a bullish formation. A double/triple bottom occurs when two/three successive lows reach approximately the same point. A double/triple bottom is considered formed when the rise from the second/third bottom moves down past the highest peak between the two/three tops. It is only then that the buy signal emerges. A double/triple top is a bearish formation. A double/triple top occurs when two/three successive highs reach approximately the same level. A double/triple top is considered formed when the fall from the second/third top moves down past the lowest point between the two/three tops. It is only then that the sell signal emerges.

Bullish market A market in which prices are expected to be rising.

Candlestick chart A type of chart in which the relationship of the opening and closing prices determines the colour of the body of the 'candle' used to depict price action on the chart. A typical candlestick consists of two parts: the real body, i.e. the rectangular part, and the shadow, i.e. the two vertical extensions from the body.

Chart A record in graphic form of market information, for example price and volume, taken at regular intervals.

Classical continuation patterns These are triangle formations, flag formations, pendant formations and rectangle formations.

Classical reversal patterns These are: head and shoulders formations; double/triple tops and bottoms formations; saucer and round top formations; spike V top and spike V bottom formations; wedge reversal formations; and island reversal formations.

Close/closing price The last traded price for the period.

Downtrend A state in which prices are steadily declining.

Dow theory An observation initiated by Charles Dow which states that:

- The averages must confirm each other.
- The averages discount everything.
- The market has three movements.
- The major trends have three phases.
- Volume must confirm the trend.
- A trend continues until the signal reverses.

S. A. Nelson (1903) wrote a book, *The ABC of Stock Speculation* on Dow theory.

Elliott wave theory A theory developed by R. N. Elliott that all market activities develop into well ordered patterns consisting of five primary waves followed by three correction waves. These principles can be found in *The Wave Principle* (1938) by Elliott.

Equivolume chart Developed by H.M. Gartley (1935), Edward Quinn and Richard Arms this involves plotting equivolume bars:

▨ The height of each equivolume bar represents the **high** and **low** traded for the period.

▨ The width of each equivolume bar represents the **volume** traded for the period.

More information can be found in Gartley (1935) *Profit in the Stock Market* and Arms (1998) *Profits in Volume: Equivolume charting*.

Equivolume chart with closing price This involves plotting a horizontal stroke as the closing price in the equivolume bar:

▨ If the closing price is higher than the previous closing price, the bar will be coloured blue and the area below the closing price will be coloured a deeper blue.

▨ If the closing price is lower than the previous closing price, the bar will be coloured red and the area above the closing price will be coloured a deeper red.

Fibonacci ratio The ratio 1.618 to 1 which may be found in many places in nature, discovered by a mathematician called Fibonacci. Starting at 1, the Fibonacci series goes 1, 1, 2, 3, 5, 8, 13, 21, 34, 55, 89, 144... where each number is the sum of the previous two numbers, and gives rise to ratios such as 144/89 = 1.618 and 89/144 = 0.618. Many believe these ratios are instrinsic to the internal order of the markets.

Fixed percentage x% (price envelope) bands system A type of band that is constructed as a certain percentage (for example 10%) around a moving average. Also known as a moving average envelope.

Flag formation A flag is a short-term congestion within narrow bands in the long-term trend. A flag is enclosed by parallel lines and is usually followed by the prevailing trend.

Fundamental analysis The study of economic information to forecast prices and gauge if an asset is overvalued or undervalued. It is the analysis of current economic data to forecast future economic conditions and calculate the fair value of an asset. It adopts an analytical approach that focuses on the underlying factors to forecast the future price of a security.

Fractal geometry An observation initiated by Benoit Mandelbrot which states that there are repeating patterns in everything from nature to time series. More information can be found in Mandelbrot and Hudson (2004) *The (Mis) Behaviour of markets, A Fractal View of Risk, Ruin and Reward.*

Gaps A breakaway gap occurs after a gap above or a gap below an extended trading range, leaving a gap with no trading activity. A common gap occurs within a trading range and does not mean anything. An exhaustion gap occurs after an extended trend and is soon followed by a reversal. A runaway gap occurs in mid-trend, after which the trend tends to accelerate faster in that direction.

High The highest price traded for the period.

Kagi chart A type of chart that records only price action without reference to time where a buy signal appears each time it moves higher than the last high and a sell signal appears each time it moves lower than the last low.

Line chart A type of chart in which a line joins up all the closing prices only.

Low The lowest price traded for the period.

Head and shoulders formation A technical chart formation consisting of three parts delineated by a neckline found at the top.

Index A data series adjusted to some base value, typically 100, as of the starting date or a given reference date. For example the FTSE 100 is an index and is used to measure the stock performance of the London Stock Exchange.

Inverse head and shoulders formation A reverse of head and shoulders formation found at the bottom.

Island bottom reversal A bullish formation. An island bottom reversal is an area where the last sellers are entering the market. The market gaps down lower on the market opening, leaving the gap unfilled (an exhaustion gap). No follow through selling occurs. The following day(s), the market gaps up, leaving the original gap unfilled. (This is a breakaway gap.)

Island top reversal formation A bearish formation. An island top reversal is an area where the last buyers are entering the market. The market gaps up higher on the market opening, leaving the gap unfilled (an exhaustion gap). No follow through buying occurs while the earlier investors have exited or are exiting the market. The following day(s), the market gaps down, leaving the original gap unfilled. (This is a breakaway gap.)

Long The state of owning a security.

Mean The average value of a data series.

Momentum A leading indicator that is calculated based on the difference between today's closing price and the closing price n days ago. Graphically, this can be depicted by a horizontal median also called the equilibrium line. When the momentum is above the equilibrium line and rising, prices are advancing with an increasing momentum. An extreme momentum reading above the equilibrium line indicates an overbought level. When the momentum is below the equilibrium line and falling, prices are falling with increasing momentum. An extreme momentum reading below the equilibrium line indicates an oversold level.

Moving average The measure of the average price (mean) of an item over the previous n periods that is recomputed each succeeding period using the most recent data.

Normal (Gaussian) distribution The natural tendency for things to be distributed in a bell-shaped curve.

On balance volume (OBV) A leading indicator developed by Woods and Vignolia and later by Joseph Granville (1963) in his book, *Granville's New Key to Stock Market Profits,* to chart an increasing cumulative volume when the price closes up and a decreasing cumulative volume when the price closes down. If volume is increasing, OBV is rising at an accelerating rate and prices are rising, this is confirmation of an uptrend. If volume is declining, OBV is rising at a decreasing rate, even though prices are rising, this is a divergence sign that the uptrend is not sustainable. If volume is increasing, OBV is falling on an accelerating rate and prices are falling, this is confirmation of a downtrend. If volume is declining, OBV is falling at a decreasing rate, even though prices are falling, this is a divergence sign that the downtrend is not sustainable.

Open interest The number of futures contracts that have been opened and have not been closed: the amount of futures contracts that are still open and in existence. For example, the open interest of London FTSE 100 futures contracts on 27/12/2010 is 653,676.

Open/opening price The price of the first trade of the period.

Optimisation The process of finding the best performing parameter for a trading system.

Orders A good-till-cancel (GTC) order is an order that is in effect until it is cancelled or when the contract expires. A limit order is an order that has a restriction on the price. A market order is an immediate execution order at the best market price. A stop order (or stop loss order) is an order to buy above the market price (or sell below the market price). A stop order becomes a market order when the stop price is triggered. It will be filled at the best available market price.

Parabolic stop and reverse (SAR) A leading indicator originated and developed by Welles Wilder to set trailing stops. In an uptrend, the dotted lines below the price are used for trailing stops. In a downtrend, the dotted lines above the price are used for trailing stops. Welles Wilder details his original technical indicators in his book, *New Concepts in Technical Trading Systems* (1978).

Parameter A value assigned to a trading system to vary/optimise the timing of the signals. For example, BBZ has two parameters that can be varied or optimised: moving average and standard deviation.

Pennant formation A pennant is like a triangle but it is a shorter-term congestion. It is enclosed by two converging lines and is usually followed by the prevailing trend.

Point and figure chart A type of chart that records only price action without reference to time using Xs and Os. Each X represents a continuous up tick while each O represents a continuous down tick.

Random walk theory An observation initiated by Eugene Fama in *Random Walks in Stock Market Prices* (1965) that states that the past history of a price series cannot be used to predict future prices in any meaningful way because prices behave in a random walk way.

Rectangle A rectangle is a trading range enclosed by two parallel lines formed by at least two tops and two bottoms.

Relative strength index (RSI) A leading indicator originated and developed by Welles Wilder that shows overbought or oversold market conditions. An RSI above 70 means the market is considered overbought. An RSI below 30 means the market is considered oversold. More information can be found in his book *New Concepts in Technical Trading Systems* (1978).

Resistance An area on a chart above the current price where identifiable trading has occurred before. It is believed that investors who bought at those higher prices will become sellers when those prices are reached again, thus halting an advance.

Rollover The closing of the current month's position and the opening of the next month's position.

Round bottom (saucer) A saucer is formed as a round bottom with a concave curve under the lows. It signals a gradual change in the market where the initial selling pressure eases to be replaced by buying pressure.

Round top A round top is formed on the top of the price series with a convex curve under the lows. It signals a gradual change in the market where the initial buying pressure eases to be replaced by selling pressure.

Short The state of being short a security. The act of selling before buying.

Slippage An order being done at a worse than expected price.

Slippage cost The cost of the difference between the hypothetical execution price and the actual price executed due to poor fill.

Standard deviation A mathematical measure of volatility that measures deviations from an average.

Stochastic A leading indicator originated and developed by George Lane that shows overbought or oversold market conditions. A stochastic above 80 means the market is considered overbought. A stochastic below 20 means the market is considered oversold. More information can be found in 'Lane's Stochastics' in the second issue of *Technical Analysis Stocks and Commodities* magazine.

Support An area where declines halt and are reversed. Support is often associated with perceived value.

Technical analysis The study of price activities or price patterns to identify trading opportunities. It is the analysis of historical price data to forecast price movements and trends. It adopts an analytical approach based on the belief that price reflects all that is knowable about a security at any given time. Therefore, the price structure itself is the best source of data for forecasting future prices.

Trading range A price range in which trading has been confined for an extended period. Generally sideways in character.

Trading range system A trading range system that initiates positions in the opposite direction of a large price movement on the assumption that the market is due for correction. A range trading system recommends selling where it perceives there is resistance and buying where it perceives there is support.

Trading rules A set of rules selected after a series of tests consisting of algorithms with optimised parameters to indicate trading signals that generate the maximum abnormal return.

Trailing stops A trailing mechanism where a GTC stop order is revised accordingly when the market is moving in the direction of the entry position.

Trend trading Trading in the overall direction of the security.

Trend trading system A trading system that initiates a position in the same direction as the current price movement on the assumption that the trend will continue.

Triangle formations An ascending triangle is usually followed by a continuation of an uptrend except for the case of triangle breakdown when a downtrend is expected to follow. A descending triangle is usually followed by a continuation of a downtrend except for the case of triangle breakout when an uptrend is expected to follow. A symmetrical triangle is usually followed by a continuation of the trend that preceded it.

Uptrend A state in which prices are steadily increasing.

V spike top/bottom V spike top/bottom is a bearish/bullish formation after an extended uptrend/downtrend where the unusual spike high/low day is above/below the highs/lows on the preceding and succeeding days. Usually, the close on the spike high/low day is nearer to the low/high of the day.

Volatility The tendency for prices to vary. Standard deviation is one measure of volatility.

Volatility breakout system A trading system designed to trigger when volatility exceeds a certain level.

Volume The number of contracts/shares traded for the period.

Volume chart A volume chart involves plotting the number of contracts traded as bars in a graph at the bottom of the price chart.

Wedge reversal formations Wedge reversal formations are found at the bottom or the top of the trend and are different from wedge continuation formations. A wedge reversal formation must be followed by a breakout of the resistance or support line in the opposite direction of the prevailing trend. A falling wedge is a bullish formation that is found at the bottom of the downtrend, when the prices converge in a downward sloping cone, followed immediately by a breakout of the resistance line into an uptrend. A rising wedge is a bearish formation that is found at the top of the uptrend, when the prices converge in an upward sloping cone, followed immediately by a breakout of the support line into a downtrend.

Whipsaw A period of wrong signals.

Z-test statistic A statistical measure to standardise the possible dispersion of values. A Z-test statistic in BBZ refers to the difference between the close and the moving average, divided by the standard deviation.

Bibliography

Achelis, S. (2000), *Technical Analysis from A to Z*, McGraw-Hill.

Alexander, S. (1961), 'Price Movements in Speculative Markets: Trends or Random Walks', *Industrial Management Review*, 2, 7–26.

Alexander, S. (1964), 'Price Movements in Speculative Markets: Trends or Random Walks No. 2.', *Industrial Management Review*, 5, 25–46.

Andersen, S., Gluzman, J.-R., and Sornette, D. (2000), 'Fundamental Framework for Technical Analysis of Market Prices', *The European Physical Journal B – Condensed Matter and Complex Systems*, 14, 3, 579–601.

Annuar Md., N., Ong, B.T. and Shamsher, M. (1995), 'Weak-Form Efficiency of the Kuala Lumpur Stock Exchange: An Application of Unit Root Analysis', *Pertanika J. Social Sciences & Humanities*, 1, 1, 56–62.

Appel, G. (2005), *Technical Analysis, Power Tools for Active Investors*, Prentice Hall.

Arms, R. (1999) *Profits in Volume: Equivolume Charting*, Marketplace Books Inc.

Azizan, N.A. (2003), 'Stock Index Futures Efficiency: Comparison Study Between Malaysia, Singapore and London', Ph.D. Dissertation, Department of Accounting and Economics, University of Liverpool.

Bachelier, L. (1900), 'Théorie de la Spéculation' (Paris: Gauthier-Villars), and reprinted in English in Paul Cootner (1964), 'The Random Character of Stock Market Prices', Cambridge: M.I.T, 1964, 17–78.

Balsara, N., Carlson, K. and Rao, N. (1996), 'Unsystematic Futures Profits with Technical Trading Rules: A Case for Flexibility', *Journal of Financial and Strategic Decisions*, 9, 1, 57–66.

Batten, J. and Ellis, C. (1996), 'Technical Trading System Performance in the Australian Share Market', *Asia Pacific Journal of Management*, 13, 1, 87–99.

Bear, R. and Stevenson, R. (1970), 'Commodity Futures: Trends or Random Walks?', *Journal of Finance*, 25, 1, 65–81.

Beja, A. and Goldman, M. (1980), 'On the Dynamic Behaviour of Prices in Disequilibrim', *Journal of Finance*, 35, 235–248.

Bessembinder, H. and Chan, K. (1995), 'The Profitability of Technical Trading Rules in Asian Stock Markets', *Pacific-Basin Finance Journal* (July), 257–284.

Bessembinder, H. and Chan, K. (1998), 'Market Efficiency and the Returns to Technical Analysis', *Financial Management*, 27, 2, 5–17.

Blume, L., Easley, D. and O'Hara, M. (1994), 'Market Stastics and Technical Analysis: The Role of Volume', *Journal of Finance*, 49, 1 (March), 153–181.

Bollinger, J. (2002), *Bollinger on Bollinger*, MacGraw Hill.

Brock, W., Lakonishok, J. and LeBaron, B. (1992), 'Simple Technical Trading Rules and The Stochastic Properties of Stock Returns', *Journal of Finance* (December), 1731–1764.

Brorsen, B. and Irwin, S. (1985), 'Public Futures Funds', *Journal of Futures Markets*, 5, 463–485.

Brorsen, B. and Irwin, S. (1987), 'Futures Funds and Price Volatility', *Review of Futures Markets*, 6, 118–135.

Campbell, J., Lo, A. and MacKinlay, A. (1997), *The Econometrics of Financial Markets*, Princeton, NJ: Princeton University Press.

Chan, J. (2005), 'Using Time Series Volatilities to Trade Trends: Trading Technique – BBZ', *Australian Technical Analysts Association Journal* (March/April 2005), 31–38.

Chan, J. (2005), *First Technical Analysis Guide*, Chan Phooi M'ng.

Chan, J. (2006), 'Trading Trends With The Bollinger Bands Z-Test', *Technical Analysis of Stocks & Commodities* (March), 46–52.

Chan, J. (2006), *Everything Technical Analysis: How to Trade Like a Professional*, Prentice-Hall.

Chan, J. (2008), *Everything Technical Analysis: How to Trade Like a Professional*, Prentice-Hall.

Chan, J. and Noor, A.A. (2009), 'Examining the Profitability of Mechanical Trading Rules Application of Standard Deviation Model, BBZ, on Kuala Lumpur Composite Futures', Proceedings, IBMA June 2009.

Chan, J. and Noor, A.A. (2010), 'Can Technical Analysis Predict the Movement of Futures Prices?', *The IUP Journal of Finance Risk Management*.

Chan, J., Ibrahim, M. and Noor, A.A. (2010), 'Adaptive Z-Test-Statistics (ABZ) Algorithm Professional Trading System – A Study on Futures Markets', *Journal of International Finance and Economics*, (June).

Chan, J., Ibrahim, M. and Noor, A.A. (2011), 'A Profitability Study on the Malaysian Futures Markets using a New Adjustable Technical Analysis Indicator ABZ', *African Journal of Business Management*.

Chande, T. (1997), *Beyond Technical Analysis: How to Develop and Implement a Winning Trading System*, John Wiley & Sons, Inc.

Chaudhuri, K. and Wu, Y. (2003), 'Random Walk Versus Breaking Trend in Stock Prices: Evidence from Emerging Markets', *Journal of Banking & Finance*, 27, 4, 575–592.

Cheung, K. and Couts, J. (2000), 'Trading Rules and Stock Returns: Some Preliminary Short Run Evidence from the Hang Seng 1985–1997', *Applied Financial Economics*, 10, 579–586.

Clyde, W and Osler, C. (1997), 'Charting: Chaos Theory in Disguise?', *Journal of Futures Markets*, 17, 489–514.

Cootner, P. (1962), 'Stock Prices: Random vs Systematic Changes', *Industrial Management Review*, 3, 24–45.

Curcio, R., Goodhart, C., Guillaume, D. and Payne, R. (1997), 'Do Technical Trading Rules Generate Profits? Conclusions from the Intra Day Foreign Exchange Market', *International Journal of Finance and Economics*, 2, 267–280.

Dacorogna, M. (1993), *The Main Ingredients of Simple Trading Models for Use in Genetic Algorithm Optimization*, Olsen & Associates.

Dacorogna, M. and Pictet, O. (1991), *A measure of Trading Model with a Risk Component*, Olsen & Associates.

Dawson, E. and Steeley, J. (2003), 'On the Existence of Visual Technical Patterns in the UK Stock Market', *Journal of Business Finance & Accounting*, 30, 263–293.

Donchian, R (1960), 'High Finance in Copper', *Financial Analysts Journal*, Nov/Dec, 133–142.

Elliott, R. (1938), *The Wave Principle*, now out of print.

Fama, E. (1965), 'Random Walks in Stock Market Prices', *Financial Analysts' Journal*, 16, 1–16.

Fama, E. (1970), 'Efficient Capital Markets: A Review of Theory and Empirical Work', *Journal of Finance*, 25, 383–417.

Fama, E. and Blume, M. (1966), 'Filter Rules and Stock market Trading', *Journal of Business*, 39, 283–306.

Fang, Y. and Xu, D. (2003), 'The Predictability of Asset Returns: An Approach Combining Technical Analysis and Time Series', *International Journal of Forecasting*, 19, 369–385.

Fernandez-Rodriquez, F., Gonzalez-Martel, C. and Sosvilla-Rivero, S. (2000), 'On the Profitability of Technical Trading Rules Based on Artificial Neural Networks: Evidence for the Madrid stock market', *Economic Letters*, 69, 89–94.

Frost, A. and Prechter, R. (2001), *Elliott Wave Principle: Key to Market Behavior*, Wiley.

Gandolfi, R., Sabatini, A. and Caselli, S. (2008), 'Dynamic MACD Standard Deviation Embedded in MACD Indicator for Accurate Adjustment to Financial Market Dynamics', *IFTA Journal*, 16–23.

Gartley. H. (ed.) (1935) *Profits in the Stock Market*, Health Research Books.

Gencay, R. (1998), 'The Predictability of Security Returns with Simple Technical Trading Rules', *Journal of Empirical Finance*, 5, 247–359.

Gencay, R. (1999), 'Linear, Non-linear and Essential Foreign Exchange Rate Prediction with Simple Technical Trading Rules', *Journal of International Economics*, 47, 91–107.

Gencay, R. and Stengos, T. (1998), 'Moving Average Rules, Volume and the Predictability of Security Returns with Feedforward Networks', *Journal of Forecasting*, 17, 401–414.

Gencay, R. and Xu, Z. (2003), 'Scaling, Self Similarity and Multifractality in FX Markets', *Physica A*, 323, 578–590.

Gleick, J. (1988), *Chaos: Making a New Science*, Wiley and Son Inc.

Granville, J. (1963), *Granville's New Key to Stock Market Profits*, Prentice Hall.

Gunasekarage, A. and Power, D. (2001), 'The Profitability of Moving Average Trading Rules in South Asian Stock Markets', *Emerging Markets Review*, 2, 17–33.

Hudson, R., Dempsey, M. and Keasey, K. (1996), 'A Note on the Weak Form Efficiency of Capital Markets: The Application of Technical Trading Rules to UK Stock Prices – 1935–1994', *Journal of Banking and Finance*, 1121–1132.

Irwin, S. and Park, C.-H. (2004), 'The Profitability of Technical Analysis: A Review', AgMAS Project Research Reports 37487.

Irwin, S. and Park, C.-H. (2009), 'A Reality Check on Technical Trading Rule Profits in the U.S. Futures Markets', *Journal of Futures Markets*, 30, 633–659.

Irwin, S. and Uhrig, J. (1984): 'Do Technical Analysts Have Holes in Their Shoes?', *Review of Research in Futures Markets*, 3, 264–277.

Ito, A. (1999), 'Profits on Technical Trading Rules and Time –Varying Expected Returns: Evidence from Pacific-Basin Equity Markets', *Pacific-Basin Finance Journal*, 7, 283–330.

Jegadeesh, N. (1990), 'Evidence of Predictable Behaviour of Security Returns', *Journal of Finance*, 45, 3, 881–898.

Jensen, M. and Benington, G. (1970), 'Random Walks and Technical Theories: Some Additional Evidence', *Journal of Finance*, 25, 469–482.

Joseph, T. (2000), 'Practical Applications of a Mechanical Trading System Using Simplified Elliot Waves Analysis' (from a website no longer available).

Kaufman, P. (1998), *Trading Systems and Methods*, John Wiley & Sons.

Lai, M.M., Balachandher Guru and Fauzias Mat Noor (2007), 'An Examination of the Random Walk Model and Technical Trading Rules in the Malaysian Stock Market', *The Malaysian Accounting Review*, 6, 2.

Leal, R. and Ratner, M. (1999), 'Test of Technical Trading Strategies in the Emerging Equity Markets of Latin America and Asia', *Journal of Banking & Finance*, 23, 1887–1905.

LeBaron, B. (1992), 'Forecast Improvements Using a Volatility Index', *Journal of Applied Econometrics*, 7, 137–150.

LeBaron, B. (1999), 'Technical Trading Rule Profitability and Foreign Exchange Intervention', *Journal of International Economics*, 49, 125–143.

Lee, C., Gleason, K. and Mathur, I. (2001), 'Trading Rule Profits in Latin American Currency Spot Rates', *International Review of Financial Analysis*, 10, 135–159.

Lento, C. (2009), 'Long Term Dependencies and the Profitability of Technical Analysis', *Institutional Research Journal of Finance and Economics*, 29, 126–133.

Lento, C. (2009), 'Volume, Variance and the Combined Signal Approach to Technical Analysis', *Journal of Money, Investment and Banking*, 7, 75–83.

Lento, C. and Gradojevic, N. (2007), 'Profitability of Technical Trading Rules: A Combined Signal Approach', *Journal of Applied Business Research*, 23, 1, 13–27.

Lequeux, P. (2001), 'Trading Style Analysis of Leveraged Currency Funds', *Journal of Asset Management*, 2, 1, 56.

Leuthold, R. (1972), 'Random Walk and Price Trends: The Live Cattle Futures Market', *Journal of Finance*, 27, 4, 879–889.

Levich, R. and Thomas, L. (1993), 'The Significance of Technical Trading Rule Profits in the Foreign Exchange Market: A Bootstrap Approach', *Journal of International Money and Finance*, 12, 451–474.

Levy, R. (1967a), 'Random Walks: Reality or Myth', *Financial Analysts' Journal*, 23, 69–77.

Levy, R. (1967b), 'Relative Strength as a Criterion for Investment Selection', *Journal of Finance*, 22, 595–610.

Levy, R. (1971), 'The Predictive Significance of Five Point Chart Patterns', *Journal of Business*, 44, 316–323.

Li, J. and Tsang, E. (1999), 'Improving Technical Analysis Predictions: An Application of Genetic Programming', Proceedings, Florida Artificial Intelligence Research Symposium, USA.

Lo, A. and MacKinlay, A. (1988), 'Stock Market Prices Do Not Follow Random Walks: Evidence From a Simple Specification Test', *Review of Financial Studies*, 1, 41–66.

Lo, A. and MacKinlay, A. (1990a), 'When are Contrarian Profits Due to Stock Market Overreaction?', *Review of Financial Studies*, 3, 176–206.

Lo, A. and MacKinlay, A. (1990b), 'Data Snooping Biases in Tests of Financial Asset Pricing Models', *Review of Financial Studies*, 3, 431–467.

Lo, A., Mamaysky, H. and Wang, J. (2000), 'Foundations of Technical Analysis: Computational Algorithms, Statistical Inference and Empirical Implementation' *Journal of Finance*, 55, 1705–1765.

Lukac, L. and Brorsen, B. (1990), 'A Comprehensive Test of Futures Market Disequilibrium', *Financial Review*, 25, 593–622.

Lukac, L., Brorsen, B. and Irwin, S. (1988a), 'A Test of Futures Market Disequilibrium Using Twelve Different Technical Trading Systems', *Applied Economics*, 20, 623–639.

Lukac, L., Brorsen, B. and Irwin, S. (1988b), 'Similarity of Computer Guided Technical Trading Systems', *Journal of Futures Markets*, 8, 1–13, 64.

Lukac, L., Brorsen, B. and Irwin, S. (1990), 'A Comparison of Twelve Technical Trading Systems', Traders Press, Inc.

Mahendra, R. (2000), 'Disequilibrium in Asia-Pacific Futures Markets: An Intra-Day Investigation', *Journal of Financial and Strategic Decisions*, 13, 2.

Maillet, B. and Michel, T. (2000), 'Further Insights on the Puzzle of Technical Analysis Profitability', *European Journal of Finance*, 6, 196–224.

Malkiel, B. (2007): 'A Random Walk Down Wall Street: The Time-tested Strategy for Successful Investing', W.W. Norton & Company, Inc.

Malliaris, A. and Urrutia, J. (1998), 'Volume and Price Relationships: Hypothesis and Testing for Agricultural Futures', *The Journal of Futures Markets*, 18, 1, 53–72.

Mandelbrot, B. (1963), 'The Variation of Certain Speculative Prices', *Journal of Business*, 36, 394–419.

Mandelbrot, B. (1967), 'The Variation of the Prices of Cotton, Wheat and Railroad Stocks and of Some Financial Rates', *The Journal of Business*, 40, 393–413.

Mandelbrot, B. (1971), 'When Can Prices be Arbitraged Efficiently? A Limit to Random Walk and Martingale Models', *Review of Economics and Statistics*, 53, 225–236.

Mandelbrot, B. (1997), 'Three Fractal Models in Finance: Discontinuity, Concentration, Risks', Economic Notes by Banca Monte del Paschi di Siena SpA, 26, 2, 171–212.

Mandelbrot, B. (2001), 'Scaling in Financial Prices I: Tails and Dependence', *Quantitative Financial*, 1, 113–123.

Mandelbrot, B. (2003), 'Heavy Tails in Finance for Independent or Multifractal Price Increments', *Handbook on Heavy Tailed Distributions in Finance*, 1, 1–31.

Mandelbrot, B. and Hudson, R. (2004), *The (Mis)Behaviour of Markets, A Fractal View of Risk, Ruin and Reward*, Profile Books Ltd.

Mandelbrot, B., Calvet, L. and Fisher, A. (1997), 'Large Deviation and the Distribution of Price Changes', Cowles Foundation Discussion Paper No 1165.

Martin, A. (2001), 'Technical Trading Rules in the Spot Foreign Exchange Markets of Developing Countries', *Journal of Multinational Financial Management*, 11, 59–68.

Mathur, I. and Szakmary, A. (1997), 'Central Bank Intervention and Trading Rule Profits in Foreign Exchange Markets', *Journal of International Money and Finance*, 16, 513–535.

Menkhoff, L. and Schlumberger, M. (1995), 'Persistent Profitability of Technical Analysis on Foreign Exchange Markets?', *Banca Nazionale del Lavoro Quarter Review*, 193, 189–216.

Metghalchi, M., Yong, G., Garza-Gomez, X. and Chen, C. (2007), 'Profitable Technical Trading Rules for the Austrian Stock Market', *International Business & Economics Research Journal*, 6, 9, 49–58.

Mills, T. (1997), 'Technical Analysis and the London Stock Exchange: Testing Trading Rules using the FT30', *International Journal of Finance and Economics*, 2, 319–331.

Murphy, A. (1986), 'Futures Fund Performance: A Test of Effectiveness of Technical Analysis', *The Journal of Futures Market*, 6, 2, 175.

Neely, C. (1997), 'Technical Analysis in the Foreign Exchange Market: A Layman's Guide', *Federal Reserve Bank of St Louis Review*, September/ October, 51–74.

Neely, C. (2002), 'The Temporal Pattern of Trading Rules Returns and Exchange Rate Intervention: Invention Does Not Generate Technical Trading Profits', *Journal of International Economics*, 58, 211–232.

Neely, C. and Weller, P. (1999), 'Technical Trading Rules in the European Monetary System', *Journal of International Money and Finance*, 18, 429–458.

Neely, C. and Weller, P. (2001), 'Technical Analysis and Central Bank Intervention', *Journal of International Money and Finance*, 20, 949–970.

Neftci, S., and Policano, A. (1984), 'Can Chartists Outperform the Market? Market Efficiency Tests for "Technical Analysis"', *The Journal of Futures Markets*, 4, 4, 465–478.

Nelson, S. A. (1903), *The ABC of Stock Speculation*, New York: S. A. Nelson.

Nicholson, C. (1998), 'What is Technical Analysis and Why Use it?', *Australian Technical Association Journal* (January/February), 1.

Oberlechner, T. (2001), 'Importance of Technical and Fundamental Analysis in The European Foreign Exchange Market', *International Journal of Finance and Economics*, 6, 1, 81–93.

Olson, D. (2004), 'Have Trading Rule Profits in the Currency Markets Declined Over Time?', *Journal of Banking & Finance*, 28, 85–105.

Papathanasious, S. and Samitas, A. (2010), 'Profits from Technical Trading Rules: The Case of Cyrus Stock Exchange', *Journal of Money, Investment and Banking*, 13.

Parker, G. and Van Horne, J. (1967), 'The Random-walk Theory: An Empirical Test', *Financial Analysts' Journal*, 23, 87–92.

Parker, G. and Van Horne, J. (1968), 'Technical Trading Rules: A Comment', *Financial Analysts Journal*, 24, 128–132.

Paulos, J. (2003), *A Mathematician Plays the Market*, Penguin Group.

Pring, M. (1991), *Technical Analysis Explained*, New York, NY: McGraw-Hill.

Querin, S. and Tomek, W. (1984), 'Random Processes in Prices and Technical Analysis', *Journal of Futures Markets*, 4, 15–23.

Quinn, E. S. (1935) 'The Economic Principles Employed in the Use and Interpretation of Trendographs' in H. Gartley (ed.) *Profits in the Stock Market*, Health Research Books.

Raj, M. and Thurston, D. (1996), 'Effectiveness of Simple Technical Trading Rules In Hong Kong Futures Markets', Applied Economics Letters, 3, 33–36.

Ratner, M. and Leal, R. (1999), 'Tests of Technical Trading Strategies in the Emerging Equity Markets of Latin America and Asia', *Journal of Banking and Finance*, 23, 1887–1905.

Saacke, P. (2002), 'Technical Analysis and the Effectiveness of Central Bank Intervention', *Journal of International Money and Finance*, 21, 459–479.

Sanjay, S. and Anurag, G. (2002), 'Abnormal Returns Using Technical Analysis: The Indian Experience', *Financial India*, 181–203.

Sapp, S. (2004), 'Are All Central Bank Interventions Created Equal? An Empirical Investigation', *Journal of Banking & Finance*, 28, 443–474.

Schleifer, A. and Summers, L. (1990), 'The Novice Trader Approach to Finance', *Journal of Economic Perspectives*, 17, 83–104.

Schoutens, W. (2003), *Levy Processes in Finance Pricing Financial Derivatives*, John Wiley & Sons Ltd.

Schwager, J. (2000), *Getting Started on Technical Analysis*, John Wiley and Sons.

Silber, W. (1994), 'Technical Trading: When It Works and When It Doesn't', *Journal of Derivatives*, 1, 39–44.

Simon, D. and Wiggins, R. (2001), 'S & P Futures Returns and Contrary Sentiment Indicators', *The Journal of Futures Markets*, 21, 5, 447–462.

Smidt, S. (1965), 'A Test of the Serial Independence of Price Changes in Soybean Futures', *Food Research Institute Studies*, 5, 117–136.

Sweeny, R. (1986), 'Beating the Foreign Exchange Market', *Journal of Finance*, 41, 163–182.

Sweeny, R. (1988), 'Some New Filter Rule Tests: Methods and Results', *Journal of Financial and Quantitative Analysis*, 23, 285–300.

Szakmary, A. and Mathur, I. (1997), 'Central Bank Intervention and Trading Rule Profits in Foreign Exchange Markets', *Journal of International Money and Finance*, 16, 513–535.

Taylor, M. and Allen, H. (1992), 'The Use of Technical Analysis in the Foreign Exchange Market', *Journal of International Money and Finance*, 11, 3, 304–314.

Taylor, S. (1986), *Modelling Financial Time Series*, John Wiley & Sons.

Taylor, S. (1992), 'Rewards Available to Currency Futures Speculators: Compensation for Risk or Evidence of Inefficient Pricing', *Economic Record*, 68, 105–116.

Taylor, S. (1994), 'Trading Futures Using A Channel Rule: A Study of The Predictive Power of Technical Analysis With Currency Examples', *Journal of Futures Markets*, 14, 215–235.

Taylor, S. (2000), 'Stock Index and Price Dynamics in the UK and the US: New Evidence for a Trading Rule and Statistical Analysis', *European Journal of Finance*, 6, 39–69.

Taylor, S. and Tari, A. (1989), 'Further Evidence Against the Efficiency of Futures Markets', in R.M.C. Guimaraes *et al.* (ed.) *A Reappraisal of the Efficiency of Financial Markets*, pp. 557–601, Springer-Verlag.

Thompson, S. and Waller, M. (1987), 'The Execution Cost of Trading in Commodity Futures Markets', *Food Research Institute Studies*, 20, 141–163.

Valcu, V. (2002), 'Z-Score Indicator', *Working Money*.

Wilder, W. (1978), 'New Concepts in Technical Trading Systems', *Trend Research*, New York.

Williams, L. (1970) *The Definitive Guide to Futures Trading* (Volume I), Windsor Books.

Williams, L. (1989) *The Definitive Guide to Futures Trading* (Volume II), Windsor Books.

Recommended websites

www.bollingerband.com

www.traders.com

www.tradingtech.com

www.turtletrader.com

http://klme2.tripod.com

www.workingmoney.com

Index

absolute range breakout xviii, 86–7
accumulation phase 102
adjustable bands Z-test statistic (ABZ)
    190–1
algorithm trading systems xix,
    106–11, 119, 132–8, 190
  design 135
  optimisation xix, 108, 135, 155
  parameters xix, 108, 135, 151
  professional trading desks 121–4
  risk to reward ratio 103, 104, 108–9,
    126, 135, 159
  robustness 108, 134, 135
  slippage xx, 110, 184
  system improvements 183
  transaction costs 110, 184
  unexpected losses 109
  whipsaws xx, 109–10, 133, 136,
    160, 184
arrogance 162
ascending triangles 39–40
ask prices 12
attitude 184
average directional index 83

backtesting xix, 134, 159, 184
bar charts 14–16
Bband Z-test statistics (BBZ) xviii, 93,
    129–30, 133–4, 147–51
  formulas 147–51
  trading rules 153
bearish engulfing sign 19
bearish primary market movements
    6–7, 8, 101
behavioural finance 181, 182

bid prices 12
black box 138
Bollinger bands 90–1, 94, 104
breakaway gap 46–7, 50
breakout *see* range breakout
bullish engulfing sign 19
bullish primary market movements
    6–7, 8, 101
buy signals
  directional movement (DM) 77
  exponential moving averages
    (EMA) 68
  moving average convergence and
    divergence (MACD) 69
  relative strength index (RSI) 75
  simple moving averages 66, 127
  stochastics 81
buy-and-hold returns 115

candlestick charts 16–19
capital preservation 135
capital requirements 160, 165–8
Chande, T. 134, 137
channels 59–60
charts xvii, 9–29
  bar 14–16
  candlestick 16–19
  constructing 12–13
  equivolume 23–8
    with closing prices 26–8
  kagi 21–3
  line 14
  OHLC 14–16
  point and figure 19–21
  and risk management 12
  volume 23

classical technical analysis 11
closing prices xvii, 12
commodity markets 140
common gap 48–9
consecutive losses 159, 166
constructing a chart 12–13
contemporary technical analysis 11
continuation patterns 39–42
    flags 41, 42
    pennants 41
    rectangles 41–2
    triangles 39–40
currency markets 140
cutting losses 3, 172

data analysis 140
day traders 7
descending triangles 39–40
designing a system 135
directional movement (DM) 76–8
    buy signals 77
    sell signals 78
discipline 162–3, 189
distribution phase 102, 103
doji sign 19
double/triple tops and bottoms 33–4
Dow, Charles 4
Dow theory xix, 6–7, 87–8, 100–5
    accumulation phase 102
    distribution phase 102, 103
    downtrend phase 103–4
    primary market movements 6–7, 8,
        101
    risk to reward ratio 103, 104
    uptrend phase 102–3
downtrends xix, 7, 55–7, 61–2, 103–4
    on balance volume (OBV) 82–3
    channels 60
downward impulse waves 97–8
dynamic volatility indicator 190

Elliott wave theory xx, 95–9
    downward impulse waves 97–8
    Fibonacci ratios 98
    stop loss orders 99
    upward impulse waves 96–7

entry and exit trading rules 160–2
envelopes see standard deviation bands
equity markets 140
equivolume charts 23–8
    with closing prices 26–8
evaluation journal 174–7
exhaustion gaps 45
exponential moving averages (EMA)
        67–8
    buy signals 68
    sell signals 68
eyeballing 151

falling wedge 37–8
falling window 50
Fama, E. 112, 113
fast trading systems 133
fat tails 144, 145
Fibonacci numbers 94, 127
Fibonacci ratios 98
fill xx
fixed percentage band breakout 87–8
flags 41, 42
formulas 146–51
fractal geometry xx, 114–15
FTSE 100 futures contract 142–4
fundamental analysis xvii, 10–11, 116
futures markets 140, 142–4, 185

Gandolfi, R. 190
gaps 44–50
    breakaway 46–7, 50
    common 48–9
    exhaustion 45
    island gap reversal 45–6
    runaway 47–8
Gartley, Harold 23
Gaussian distribution 113, 114
good-till-cancel (GTC) orders 131,
        170–1, 189

head and shoulders 31–3
herd mentality 181
highest prices xvii, 12
Hudson, R. 115

indicators *see* technical indicators
intrinsic value 10
inverse head and shoulders 32
Irwin, S. 115, 140
island gap reversal 45–6

journals *see* record keeping

kagi charts 21–3

lagging indicators 64–71
leading indicators 72–84, 135
    average directional index 83
    on balance volume (OBV) 81–3, 84
    directional movement (DM) 76–8
    momentum 73–4, 83
    parabolic stop and reverse 78–9, 83
    relative strength index (RSI) 74–6, 83
    stochastics 79–80, 83
leverage 142–3, 185
limit orders 130–1
line charts 14
linear trading 162, 163, 189
liquid markets 110
live testing 134
long positions xx
    parabolic stop and reverse 79
long white/black candlestick 18
losing trade ratio 135–6
loss aversion 182
losses 122–3, 124, 154–5
    consecutive 159, 166
    cutting 3, 172
    evaluation journal 175–6
    maximum 168
    probability of losing 163–4, 166–7
    see also stop loss orders
lowest prices xvii, 12

Mandelbrot, B. 114–15
margin payments 122–3, 142–3,
    154–5, 160
market characteristics 140–1
mathematical formulas 146–51
maximum losses 168
mechanical trading xix, 60, 62, 121,
    125–6

model trading *see* algorithm trading
    systems
momentum 73–4, 83
moving averages xviii, 65–6, 70–1,
    126–8, 147–51
    buy signals 66, 69, 127
    choosing number of days 127–8
    convergence and divergence
        (MACD) xviii, 68–9
    exponential (EMA) 67–8
    range breakout 87–8, 94
    sell signals 66, 69, 127
    trading rules 153

narrow shapes 25
neckline 31
noise 188–9

OHLC charts 14–16
on balance volume (OBV) 81–3,
    82–3, 84
open interest xvii, 12
opening prices xvii, 12
optimisation xix, 108, 135, 155
    Bband Z-test statistics (BBZ) xviii
oscillators 73, 83
overconfidence 182
oversquare shapes 25
overtrading 162

parabolic stop and reverse 78–9, 83
parameters xix, 108, 135
    changing 151
Park, C.-H. 115, 140
patterns 10, 11, 30–43
    continuation patterns 39–42
    double/triple tops and bottoms 33–4
    flags 41, 42
    head and shoulders 31–3
    pennants 41
    rectangles 41–2
    reversal patterns 19, 31–8
    rounded tops and bottoms 35
    triangles 39–40
    V spike tops and bottoms 35–7
    wedge reversals 37–8

pennants 41
perfect trading systems 156
planning 3, 8, 157–64
    capital requirements 160, 165–8
    components 158
    entry and exit trading rules 160–2
    following a plan 162–3
    linear trading 162, 163, 189
    overtrading 162
    pyramiding 162
    risk to reward ratio 103, 104, 108–9,
        126, 135, 159
    strategies 158–9, 163
    writing a plan 160–2
point and figure charts 19–21
post-mortem evaluations 174
power law 115
power shapes 25
price envelopes 53, 55, 87–8
    see also standard deviation bands
price patterns see patterns
primary market movements 6–7, 8, 101
probability of winning/losing 163–4,
        166–7
products 142–4
professional traders 119–24
professional trading desks 121–4
profit analysis 124, 154–5
    evaluation journal 176–7
    probability of winning 163–4, 166–7
Profits in the Stock Market 23
Profits in Volume: Equivolume Charting
        23
psychology 178–82
pyramiding 162

Quinn, Edward S. 23

random walk theory xx, 112–16
range breakout 50, 85–94, 87–8, 94,
        129–30
    absolute range breakout xviii, 86–7
    Bollinger bands 90–1, 94, 104
    fixed percentage band breakout 87–8

price envelopes 87–8
    volatility breakout 92–3, 129–30
range trading xviii, 7, 52, 63, 110
    data analysis 140
    price envelope bands 53, 55
    resistance xviii, 54–5
    support xviii, 52–3
    volatility 91
    whipsaws 136
record keeping 173–7
    actual and permissible losses 175–6
    actual and projected profit 176–7
    post-mortem evaluations 174
rectangles 41–2
relative strength index (RSI) 74–6, 83
    buy signals 75
    sell signals 75
research 139–45, 185–6, 188
    data analysis 140
    market characteristics 140–1
    products 142–4
resistance xviii, 54–5
reversal patterns 19, 31–8
    double/triple tops and bottoms 33–4
    head and shoulders 31–3
    rounded tops and bottoms 35
    V spike tops and bottoms 35–7
    wedge reversals 37–8
rising wedge 37–8
rising window 50
risk management 12
    see also stop loss orders
risk to reward ratio 103, 104, 108–9,
        126, 135, 159
robustness 108, 134, 135
rollover xx, 184
rounded tops and bottoms 35
runaway gap 47–8

scalpers 7, 161, 164
secondary corrections 6, 8
sell signals
    directional movement (DM) 78
    exponential moving averages
        (EMA) 68

moving average convergence and
    divergence (MACD) 69
relative strength index (RSI) 75
simple moving averages 66, 127
stochastics 81
short positions xx
parabolic stop and reverse 79
slippage xx, 110, 184
slow trading systems 134
spreadsheets 146–51
square shapes 25
standard deviation bands xviii, 57, 59,
    89–90, 93, 126, 129–30, 133–4
adjustable 190–1
formulas 147–51
trading rules 153
see also price envelopes
stochastics 79–80, 83
buy signals 81
sell signals 81
stock markets 140
stop loss orders 99, 107, 119, 136,
    159, 161, 169–72
good-till-cancel (GTC) 131, 170–1,
    189
revealing to others 164
trailing stops 162, 171–2
strategies 158–9, 163
support xviii, 52–3
symmetrical triangles 39–40
system improvements 183

technical analysis xvii, 3–4
definitions 10–11
technical indicators xviii, 64–84,
    125–31
average directional index 83
on balance volume (OBV) 81–3, 84
Bband Z-test statistics (BBZ) xviii,
    93, 129–30, 133–4, 147–51
directional movement (DM) 76–8
exponential moving averages (EMA)
    67–8
lagging indicators 64–71
leading indicators 72–84, 135
momentum 73–4, 83

moving averages xviii, 65–6, 70–1,
    126–8, 147–51
convergence and divergence xviii,
    68–9
parabolic stop and reverse 78–9, 83
relative strength index (RSI) 74–6, 83
stochastics 79–80, 83
test results 141, 153–5
backtesting xix, 134, 159, 184
live testing 134
theories xix–xx
Dow theory xix, 6–7, 87–8, 100–5
Elliott wave theory xx, 95–9
fractal geometry xx
random walk theory xx, 112–16
tipsters 29, 180
trade evaluations 174
trading plans see planning
trading psychology 178–82
trading range see range trading
trading rules 152–6, 188–91
Bband Z test statistics (BBZ) 153
entry and exit trading rules 160–2
moving averages 153
trading strategies 158–9
trading terms 7
trailing stops 162, 171–2
transaction costs 110, 184
trend trading 55–63, 110, 134–7, 158
on balance volume (OBV) 82–3
channels 59–60
data analysis 140
downtrends xix, 7, 55–7, 61–2, 82–3
fast trading systems 133
mechanical systems xix, 60, 62
problems with 133–4
slow trading systems 134
standard deviation bands 57, 59,
    126, 129–30
uptrends xix, 7, 57–9, 62, 82–3
volatility xx, 89–90, 91, 92
whipsaws xx, 109–10, 133, 136,
    160, 184
triangles 39–40
triple tops and bottoms 33–4

unexpected losses 109
uptrends xix, 7, 57–9, 62, 102–3
    on balance volume (OBV) 82–3
    channels 59
upward impulse waves 96–7

V spike tops and bottoms 35–7
variance 89
volatility xx, 89–90, 91, 92
    dynamic volatility indicator 190
volatility breakout 92–3, 129–30
volume xvii, 7, 12
    on balance volume (OBV) 82–3, 84
    equivolume charts 23–8

Wall Street Journal 4
wave theory *see* Elliott wave theory
wedge reversals 37–8
whipsaws xx, 109–10, 133, 136, 160,
    184
winning psychology 178–82
winning trade ratio 135–6
writing a plan 160–2

Z-test statistic 147–50
    adjustable bands 190–1
    Bband (BBZ) xviii, 93, 129–30,
        133–4, 147–51, 153

Printed in Great Britain
by Amazon